THE WEIGHTED FEATHER

THE WEIGHTED FEATHER

Essays for Alchemical Living & Empowering Mindfulness

JULIE J. HIGHTMAN

FAIZ

Julie J. Hightman

Copyright

"This book is dedicated to all those I have shared life with and witnessed in the journey of expanding mindfulness. Thank you for your love, laughter, tears, and wisdom. "

Contents

"Remaking the World"   xi

A Letter from the Author   xv

Introduction: Becoming the Authentic Self   xvii

I   The Interdependence of Morale, Mortality, and Immortality   1

II   How Expectations Define Our Perceptions of the World   7

III   Projection and How We Affect What We Manifest   11

IV   Discerning Projection and Healthy Communication   16

V   The Relationship Between Confidence and Motivation   20

VI   Creativity and Self-Care   24

VII   How Fear and Love affect Free Will   28

VIII   Consumption: Guilt, Resentment, and Regret   33

IX   The Faces of Humility   38

X   Devotion in Love   42

XI   How We Connect & Define a Sense of Loyalty   46

XII   When Self-Entitlement Becomes Self-Sabotage   50

XIII   Compassionate Communication for Conflict
Resolution   55

XIV   Being a Witness and Experiencing the Synchrony
of Life   59

XV   Empowered Humility and Adaptability   64

XVI   Finding Your Center Within the Duality of Mind
and Life   67

XVII   Validation in Personal Values and Becoming the
Authentic Self   71

XVIII   Harnessing the Senses   75

XIX   Integrity and Leading with Intention   79

XX   The Power of Acknowledgment   83

XXI   The Constellation Effect in Self and Relationships   87

XXII   Soul Contracts and Closure Beyond Grief and
Loss   91

XXIII   Vulnerability and Resilience with an Open Heart   95

XXIV   Honorable Transparency, Truth, and Lying   99

XXV   On Worthiness   103

XXVI   Lightheartedness in Times of Hardship   107

MEDITATIONS FOR PERSONAL HEALING & EMPOWERMENT

XXVII   Lotus Blessings Empowerment Meditation   116

XXVIII Meditation for Aligning with Gratitude for your
Earthen Body   118

XXIX Meditation for Building Self-Trust   121

XXX Meditation for Being One with your Authentic
Self   123

XXXI Rainbow Light Infusion Meditation   125

XXXII Meditation for Graceful Acceptance   127

About the Author: Then to Now   131

"Remaking the World"

Creation Story from Brule Sioux Tribe

Documented by Richard Erdoes and Alfonso Ortiz in American Indian Myths and Legends

There was a world before this world, but the people in it did not know how to behave themselves or how to act human. The creating power was not pleased with that earlier world. He said to himself: " I will make a new world." He had a pipe bag and the chief pipe, which he put on the pipe rack which he had made in the sacred manner. He took four dry buffalo chips, placed three of them under the three sticks, and saved the fourth one to light the pipe.

The Creating Power said to himself: " I will sing three songs, which will bring a heavy rain. Then I'll sing a fourth song and stamp four times on the earth, and the earth will crack wide open. Water will come out of the cracks and cover all the land." When he sang the first song, it started to rain. When he sang the second, it poured. When he sang the third, the rain swollen rivers overflowed their beds. But when he sang the fourth song and stamped on the earth, it split open in many places like a shattered gourd, and water flowed from the cracks until it covered everything.

The Creating Power floated on the sacred pipe and on his huge pipe bag. He let himself be carried by waves and wind this way and that, shifting for a long time. At last the rain stopped, and by then all the people and animals had drowned. Only Kangi, the crow, survived, though it had no place to rest and was very tired. Flying above the pipe, "Tunka-shila, Grandfather, I must soon rest"; and three times the crow asked him to make a place for it to land.

The Creating Power thought:" Its time to unwrap the pipe and open the pipe bag." The wrapping and the pipe bag contained all manner of animals and birds, from which he selected four animals known for their ability to stay under water for a long time. First he sang a song and took the loon out of the bag. He commanded the loon to dive and bring a lump of mud. The loon did dive, but it brought up nothing. "I dived and dived but couldn't reach bottom," the loon said. "I almost died. The water is too deep."

The Creating Power sang a second song and took the otter out of the bag. He ordered the otter to dive and bring up some mud. The sleek otter at once dived into the water, using its strong webbed feet to go down, down, down. It was submerged for a long time, but when it finally came to the surface, it brought nothing.

Taking the beaver out of the pipe's wrapping, the Creating Power sang a third song. He commanded the beaver to go down deep below the water and bring some mud. The beaver thrust itself into the water, using its great flat tail to propel itself downward. It stayed under water longer than the others, but when it finally came up again, it too brought nothing.

At last the Creating Power sang the fourth song and took the turtle out of the bag. The turtle is very strong. Among our people it stands for long life and endurance and the power to survive. A turtle heart is great medicine, for it keeps on beating a long time after the turtle is dead. " You must bring the mud," the Creating Power told the turtle. It dove into the water and stayed below so long that the other three animals shouted: " The turtle is dead, it will never come up again!" All the time, the crow was flying around and begging for a place to land.

After what seemed to be eons, the turtle broke the surface of the water and paddled to the Creating Power. "I got to the bottom!" the turtle cried. "I brought some earth!" And sure enough, its feet and claws, and even the space in the cracks on its sides between its upper and lower shell were filled with mud.

Scooping mud from the turtles feet and sides, the Creating Power began to sing. He sang all the while that he shaped the mud in his hands and spread it on the water to make a spot of dry land for himself. When he had sung the fourth song, there was enough land for the Creating Power and for the crow. "Come down and rest," said the Creating Power to the crow, and the bird was glad.

Then the Creating Power took from his bag two long wing feathers of the eagle. He waved them over his plot of ground and commanded it to spread until it covered everything. Soon all the water was replaced by earth. "Water without earth is not good," thought the Creating Power, "but land without water is no good either." Feeling pity for the land, he wept for the earth and the creatures he would put upon it, and his tears became oceans, streams, and lakes. "That's better," he thought.

Out of his pipe bag the Creating Power took all kinds of animals, birds, plants, and scattered them over the land. When he stamped on the earth, they all came alive. From the earth the Creating Power formed the shapes of men and women. He used the red earth and white earth, black earth, and yellow earth, and made as many as he thought would do for a start. He stamped on the earth, and the shapes came alive, each taking the color of the earth out of which it was made. The Creating Power said to them: "The first world I made was bad; the creatures on it were bad. So I burned it up. The second world I made was bad too, so I drowned it. This is the third world I have made. Look: I have created a rainbow for you as a sign that there will be no more Great Flood. Whenever you see a rainbow, you will know that it has stopped raining."

The Creating Power continued: "Now, if you have learned how to behave like human beings and how to live in peace with each other and with other living things-- the two-legged, the four-legged, the many legged, the fliers, the no-legs, the green plants of this universe-- then all will be well. But if you make this world bad and ugly, then I will destroy this world too. Its up to you"

The Creating Power gave the people the pipe. "Live by it," he said. He named this land the Turtle Continent because it was there that the turtle came up with the mud out of which the third world was made. "Someday there might be a fourth world," the Creating Power thought." Then, he rested.

Told by Leonard Crow Dog at Grass Mountain,
Rosebud Indian Reservation 1974

A Letter from the Author

This book was written for the minds and hearts of individuals seeking mindfulness and provocative considerations that support them in their intentions for holistic fulfillment. The essays in this book open a journey into self-awareness and refine questions and perceptions one is cultivating or reviewing. Each concept is like an oyster bed filled with many pearls. My advice as the author is to take your time when drinking in the thoughts. Meditate on what resonates. This means reflecting in what already aligns in the perceptions of self, behaviors, and experiences as well as what feels harder to grasp, accept, or offer consideration to.

All emotions and thoughts are valid because they appear as a guidelight to seeing deeper connections within one's personal associations to the narrative they have experienced, are actively living, and intend to create. The origin of truth is always found within once we refine the path to unfold it. The closer we are to this sense of truth that aligns in the core of self, the more we trust ourselves to make choices that lead to more fulfilling outcomes. This is the path of sovereignty. It is the journey of becoming the authentic self in harmonious balance with our relationships to "other" in the world.

Building loyalty with the authentic self supports the integrity and skills we have the capacity to embody. Integrity requires consistent honesty and accountability with self and others. One may aspire or idealize about self in the mind but authentic truths only endure when choices and behaviors reveal actualized integrity and embodiment of them. Embracing vulnerability and giving oneself permission to deepen understanding in the fabric of emotions and thoughts interconnecting bestows clarity in how one is designed. This clarity establishes opportunity for healthy autonomy, which potentiates the strength to be *seen* by others honoring their own integrity for mutual exchange.

How do you want to live life? How do you want to perceive yourself when you reflect on your choices in life as a legacy? The experiences of life offer us many paths of transformation. Cyclical patterns that are learned and witnessed may subject one to a sense of impotence. They may also be shifted, released, and redesigned when one aspires to the release of karma and the cultivation of alchemy within.

May the passion in your blood, the wisdom in your bones, and the illumination of your essence be your closest allies in the navigation of your own personal narrative.

May the passages in these pages open the door to the vast networks of mindful living and support you in the more graceful acquisitions of holistic fulfillment for your incarnate soul.

In Harmony,
Julie J Hightman

Introduction: Becoming the Authentic Self

In Egyptian lore, Anubis, the God of the Dead stands at the gateway to the spirit world with his scales to weigh the soul. The scale of souls is balanced by the weight of a feather to assess the lightness a soul has attained. The degree of light attained in one's being is dependent on the integrity and truth they embody in alignment with their authentic self. The vibrational purity of this authentic self resonates in every circumstance throughout the journey of a life to activate and influence the cultivation of en-lighten-ment. This path of enlightenment unveils the keys to personal empowerment, release from karmic bondage, and profound wisdom in the connectivity of all things.

The word enlightenment represents the concept of finding lightness in the meaning of self and the meaning of life. Harnessing the potency of this lightness is achieved within the alchemy of suffering and healing, of creation and death, of the known and the unknown. The expansion of awareness may be constructed in many ways. That is why the sages speak of "1000-fold" or "infinite" paths to reaching enlightenment. These paths have many peaks and valleys with frequent diverging and converging crossroads. Every soul comes into body with their own unique design that aligns them to the core programs of their own authentic self, as well as the threads in the vast fabric of the universal authentic self. In the warp and weft of the individual and universal authenticity, the offerings of harmony and fulfillment are defined. Peeling back the layers of perception and unwinding the threads of belief reveals the solid or hollow core of truth, including the operable value of its structure when intact.

Alchemy is a physical and meta-physical process. Billions of atoms dance in and out of time and space to form, to merge, to bond, and to transform in the creation of matter, as we know it. What is matter? What does it matter? Matter is meaning and a lack of meaning, waiting to be perceived. All thoughts, emotions, and actions represent what "matter" is within and how "what matters" is directed or contained for use in our internal and external world of experience. The natural process of existence is alchemical. This includes the path of humanity and the path of the soul. Acknowledging and embracing the opportunity to engage in the alchemy of life, by choice, further inspires curiosity and enthusiasm for the magic in the mystery we all feel deep within. Even without acknowledgment, the alchemical synchrony of one's path persists beneath the veils of awareness. This inherent truth of the authentic self is always present and interactive in the behavioral responses, mental tapes, emotional defaults, and circumstantial outcomes in an individual's life narrative. When we align our choices with the authentic self, we feel strength through clarity and a dynamic flow that resonates with wholeness. When we do not align, we feel a sense of weakness, clouds of distortion that obscure our intention, and a divide with genuine integrity.

To seek the path of enlightenment is to seek empowerment in the will to co-create one's life narrative. This requires skill in the wielding of mindful awareness, a balance of responsibility, intentional manifestation, and surrender by actively witnessing the patterns of self, others, and the world. With this knowledge comes the opportunity to re-align and re-design the cyclical experiences and outcomes that feel confining, destructive, and unfulfilling, while magnifying the frequency of freedom, perpetual wholeness, and harmonic fulfillment. Becoming one with the authentic self may take many lives or events that challenge the mind, heart, and spirit to heal and lighten, beyond the weight of suffering. It may require the soul to face many paths of illusion that threaten to disconnect the nourishing origins and creative capacity of the authentic self. This causes pressure on one's integrity, the confidence to know truth, and to harness the power of intention within. Within darkness is the seed of light. Within light there is the seed of darkness. Both are integral to the balance of time and space, of birth and death, of life's losses and achievements. This interdependent relationship perpetuates possibility. It perpetuates what matters and what has yet to be understood as mattering. This means possibility is constructed upon a cycle of sustainability, based in the concept of alchemical rebirth.

Alchemical living honors the existence of the authentic self and embarks upon the journey to discover it. Those that choose to align with their own authenticity and the universal authenticity share this integrity with the world, creating an invitation for others to align in their authentic self with shared transparency and accountability. This shared meeting of inherent value, in the experience of an individual, advocates respect and compassion when co-creating relationship and pursuing successful outcomes in life. Focusing effort and intention in the agreements we make with others and ourselves unlocks the expansive capacity for creative fulfillment in our endeavors, healing from perceived wounds, and untying karmic patterns that may dictate personal perceptions or the outcomes in our personal narrative. Through this effort we learn new ways to act with greater presence for what we align and create. Through practice these skills for transparency and presence become entrained and embodied, requiring less effort. The dance in the garden of life becomes lighter and brighter and the weight of the soul hovers on the scale of Anubis without fear or resistance to being seen.

I

❦

The Interdependence of Morale, Mortality, and Immortality

Many would argue that faith and belief are the cause of one's resilience or dis-empowerment to the point of despair. When spirituality and science vie for the lead in one's mind, creating clarity or obscurity in truth and fallacy, one's rationalizations are often compartmentalized without full integration. The rules we perceive in life are founded in our orientation to the contexts of living. These rules are also influenced by the responses of others we witness interacting with life in their own way. If someone is no longer able to be a witness of others, they lose the objective input that is inherent in the awareness of other stories, practices, and responses that teach or influence us into another state of creativity. Creativity is what revitalizes our morale and our perspectives on mortality.

If we lose the witness of self we lose the objective awareness of our own subjectivity and become immersed only in the experience of subjective perceptions. Any further actions we make for the good of self, in the face of self, or in the face of circumstance is obscured due to this limiting perspective. The maintenance of both forms of awareness allows the creative mind to ask questions that expand perceptions. This cultivates new possibilities that may benefit greater acceptance of how self operates in the world. This is directly applicable to experiences that challenge morality and mortality. When one feels a loss or a diminishing of passion, the perception of will is intertwined with resilience or defeat. Actively seeking out love and connection for reflection and playtime to re-invigorate release is an essential asset in the enlightenment of our passion within. Resilience and defeat may still operate as feelings within self but be transformed into "something" more expansive and less confining subjectively. This "operable something" may arise in specific contexts or from a consistent belief we apply, but both are influenced and substantiated by creativity. Creativity is a skillful power led by the re-enlightened passion that loving connection and play have to offer.

Every day is a new day to choose how we want to orient ourselves to the experience of existence. One can choose an open heart with gratitude and graceful strength or any other emotional box of resistance. The choice to expand or contract is there in every moment. How we carry our accountability around our receptivity and willingness to resolve the dissonance or to be the dissonance during times of hardship affects our integrity of self and our integrity with others. It also affects the outcome of circumstances and may be the key that opens or shuts doors in the material world we seek to manifest our dreams in and the psyche we exist in. The stronger the resistance and dissonance we choose, the more walls we construct because creativity within must be used. Understanding that our mental and emotional programs offer us choice and the use of our creative will to navigate our inner and outer world, emphasizes the need for attention to our intentions and the integrity of our choices.

We are co-creative beings living together in the same planet, community, and/or family. We affect one another by the choices we make. When we are affected by the choices of others, we must consider our own choices in how to orchestrate a response for an intentional outcome. The choice within self is always present in every circumstance. Even when we feel helpless or without control, one can choose how to creatively transform the void or the excess in a harmonious way by acknowledging the spark of life we carry at the core of mortality.

We all have wounds and experiences that challenge our desire and will to maintain an open heart. Some wounds heal more quickly than others. Some wounds scar and remain as a reminder of something we have yet to work through. These wounds can feel picked at and reopened when similar circumstances arise to challenge our capacity for creative response. Other wounds remain open, weeping and swelling, demanding our constant attention and increasing our sensitivity to many things, related or unrelated to the wound. This happens because pain demands attention and consumes the mind as a protective measure from further injury.

Vulnerability is experienced when we are concerned with protection of self and protection of our wounds. Vulnerability is also experienced when we seek intimacy and deeper connection with others. How do we navigate the sense of vulnerability effectively to achieve the intimacy we seek in the shared experience of creation when we are wounded? So many programs and rules layer on top of one another with each experience, with each healed or unhealed wound. Our resistance builds walls like a maze that our psyche travels through each day. Is it a sanctuary or a prison? Are the walls full of mirrors or windows? Perhaps neither. Do we lash out at others or lash in at ourselves to prove the will we still have to direct and affect with?

Vulnerability requires a delicate balance of self-protection and open heartedness. It requires open mindedness to new experiences and steady caution while navigating these experiences. When we embrace the creative spark within and acknowledge our will to direct that passion in a generous way, we must also open our beingness to receive. This mutual exchange is the merit of the experience. The details of giving and receiving may look differently than we expect due to the roles we take on circumstantially. Regardless of these differences, a co-creative spark is motivated and an opportunity to integrate deeper wisdom in healing our wounds manifests greater intimacy with our self and others. The healing of a wound may require many things by the mind, but the soul only requires acknowledgment of its' creative fire. At the highest degree of intimacy, the heart seeks the reflection of that soulful fire. It is essential to embrace deconstruction as a tool in order to know how to let go of a dream, a belief, and/or a wound. Letting go enables a cathartic release of passion. By deconstructing we learn how to reconstruct and align more intimately the capacity for will, passion, vulnerability, and play that we innately carry in our sense of mortality and immortality.

Creativity may be used in constructive and deconstructive ways within the psyche of self and the choices we make to define, design, and refine the life we experience. The experience of real or metaphorical death can be equally profound. Either engage us to initiate a process of reflection, refinement, and transformation by drawing on the well of inner creativity. We are the architects and the engineers working out the questions and negotiating contracts to build our dreams in order to sustain the sacredness of our body, heart, and mind in the material world. Every relationship, every venture is a choice to seek out, to maintain, to transform, or to release. Our analysis of its purpose, how it serves us, and how we serve it is essential to working out the design. Deconstructing our expectations and hypotheses is a part of perfecting our skillset to utilize the creative force within that is fed by the essence of immortality. Dismantling and discarding all or part of a constructed idea, belief, relationship, or life may be necessary as a path to greater understanding and integration. By doing so, an expanded view for improvement is enabled that inspires the passion to dream and manifest and dream and manifest, etc.

If an individual is in alignment with the dynamic cycles of creation potentiating the forge of passion and directing the strength of will beyond stagnation and catharsis, vulnerability becomes a gentle dance of trust. This trust is founded in the acknowledgment of what animates the soul and the experience of beingness. This is the "something" transformed in every moment enabled by the seed of creativity. It is the origin of all thoughts and emotions. The choice to say "yes" to life and death, as gateways to new opportunities, is the choice to be vulnerable. Life and death open the doorways to intimacy with self and others through the nature of our mammalian imprinting and motivation to understand the experience of existence. Through this perpetuation of "inspire-ation" and acknowledgment of the exchange intimacy gifts to us, the confidence and trust in our own capacity to heal and renew our passions is instilled.

-When you are losing morale and your inspiration is waning, seek the reconnection of your creative soul to the engineer of the mind. When you are questioning mortality and feel lost in obscurity, seek the reconnection of your heart and soul to the co-creation of intimacy. Clarify and redesign your art of play and your work of dreams with the eye of the immortal architect.~

II

How Expectations Define Our Perceptions of the World

The impulse for expectations and ideals is automatic in our experience of the world. From a young age and throughout life we define our expectations by how we are treated and what is given or taken from us. This inherent aspect of beingness is not only mental construct. It is also instinctual. The basic needs for survival are an instinctual craving and expectation to be fulfilled by oneself or others. Idealistic expectations, standards, or imposed requirements for life beyond basic needs evolve from one of the most beautiful parts of our minds; inspiration, the desire to create. This attribute of humanness is a drive that has need of fortification and perpetuation, in order to sustain a sense of contentment about living. You could say it's about being more than the instinctual animal self that most would define as "humanity."

In our efforts to create our vision or ideal we define expectations of ourselves, of others, and of the world. How well we keep our agreements and meet those expectations and how others or the world do or do not, greatly affects our perceptions of the experience. The outcome or continued struggle affects the narrative we carry about ourselves, others, and the event. When one seeks to have an affect to feel fulfilled the fixation on control and the conflict of what we have control over arises. Have we assessed the motive of our expectations? Do we need or do we want to have these expectations met? And how much control do we have over the outcome? These questions must be asked internally in the trivial moments of going to the store for an item you plan to purchase and it being unavailable, to the moments in a relationship when someone is saying or doing something that doesn't feel good or enough for you, to the moment of putting all one's efforts on a job promotion and achieving it.

If we all have expectation, inspired ideals, needs, and wants in this world, then we all are co-creating our experience. Control becomes less and less broad in our understanding of how others and the world will fulfill our expectations and more fine tuned to how we can use control to work out our own ability to fulfill basic needs and ideals or to release disappointment that arises from their lack of fulfillment. Self-control can offer us a moment to step back and re-assess if we understand what it is that is unfulfilled. The same creative inspiration that defines expectation may be reworked to a concept that is more attainable or dissolved altogether if it isn't serving us emotionally and mentally. Thoughts of expectation, control, need, and how we perceive the world are deeply intertwined in the optimism or pessimism one obtains in each situation.

Remembering to have compassion for self and others with the understanding that we are all working out the experience of expectations, met and unmet, offers the opportunity to discuss our perceptions of a situation in productive ways. This opportunity to share is essential to letting go of the need to control others or the world around us and to honor the co-creativity we have the power to learn from, heal from, be served by, and achieve with. Learning to recognize the balance of personal authority requires releasing the need for control over others and expectations of others to live by our desires. It is beneficial for oneself and others to create fulfilling connection with less need for control and expectations of others to live by our desires. It is not about having high or low expectations. It is about needs and desires. It is about making requests and communicating those needs and desires to give them a clear opportunity to be met and honored as a "co-creative contract." Many expectations focus on the external world to satisfy something inside oneself. The co-creative contract may be applied directly to conversations and agreements when processing inner conflicts of the ego experience and the deeper center of one's true nature within. This is in regard to our perceptions of the world and our "way" in it.

Humility is a teacher. It is a core element of adaptability. The balance between humility and ambition must be reached to surrender oneself to the forces of life and love, and to feel the rhythmic dance of being "one with the flow." Expectations are intimately connected to trust. When expectations are met, trust is strengthened. When they are not, trust is lost to any lesser or greater degree. This connection of trust and expectation is reliant on the awareness and the communication of basic needs and ideals. One must have accountability in their communication to have integrity and refined clarity in the outcomes of expectations met or unmet that affect their perceptions of the world and their own personal narrative.

Over time the erosion of trust and the inflation of trust may result in illusion. The illusion grows by our attachments to the outcomes of our expectations. This is why many spiritual practices teach trust without attachment to expectation and humility for what is given and what is taken.

A sense of harmony and subdued suffering is possible when one releases attachment to expectation, by defining what is unnecessary or detrimental in the imprints of experiential outcomes. These factors influence and dictate how one seeks fulfillment in the world. The invitation is to practice less attachment and to be a witness of self, others, and the nature of existence. It is natural to have expectations and attachments. Finding the balance of acting and yielding in our co-creativity is the way to perpetuate dynamic flow beyond the resistance of disappointment and the ebb and flow of our perceived success. This flow opens the opportunity to learn, to expand, to re-define, and re-potentiate in our creation, by the perceptions of our expectations.

~Expectations have the power to fortify us in productive ways and to impede our progress in confining ways. Our perceptions of ourselves, others, and the world are immersed in our attachments for what we invite in and how we choose to actively or passively engage in the experience of every day.~

III

❦

Projection and How We Affect What We Manifest

Projection of the mind is a part of everyday life. As cerebral beings we are programmed to receive information, formulate structures for that information through analysis and organization, then manifest action from those structures. Projection is a tenuous and many times inaccurate process as we assess and fine tune our thoughts, emotions, and beliefs, enacting them in our endeavors of existence. This occurs in the hierarchy of conscious states from survival mode to greater opportunities to live beyond primary needs, shifting ones focus more and more to expanding thoughts in ideals and away from basic struggles for the security of food and shelter. Projection can act to manifest outcomes in an individual's life that perpetuate or shift a narrative that creates harmony or conflict. Once externalized, these projections affect our relationship to goals and connection with others. Understanding how projection is a major factor in every moment of our experience is essential to recognizing how our projections, clear or distorted, are serving or hurting us in our everyday life.

Awareness of self is an essential task and a skill to be cultivated for mastery of progressive fulfillment in our perceptions of self, relationship with others, and accomplishments in the world. Fine-tuning our awareness requires dedication and effort to evolve with greater efficiency in our analysis of information and the structures of belief we exist in and act from. When we turn our attention to the multidimensional concept of projection, it is like stepping into a maze of mirrors. Each reflection is a projection of self as it is, as it could be, and as one believes it should be. Then there are the reflections of possibility for how to receive and how to respond to each circumstance while the input of information from our experience is coming through. The program breaks down and defines the direction to lead our thoughts, emotions, and actions forward to manifest the next outcome in the narrative. The hall of mirrors can be an overwhelming place, inciting fear and frustration that can be entrapping or too much to even enter, at all. Individuals that struggle with introspection, sorting, organizing, and coordinating the impulses that are innate to human thought and emotion will become trapped here.

Resistance is a natural factor in the process of evolution. Resistance will arise as a subtle or intense pressure depending on the capacity of every individual to filter, sort, and organize their external life circumstances and internal perceptions of self within those circumstances. Whether or not one chooses to acknowledge projection as a gear in the mechanism of their life, resistance will exist. Expanding one's clarity of how projections of self, others, and the circumstances one faces can reduce the experience of resistance. Activating this awareness protects and balances the amount of resistance from one's own projected perceptions that affect the outcomes and repeat storylines in their personal narrative. Projection can act to manifest outcomes in an individual's life that perpetuate or shift a narrative creating harmony or conflict. Once externalized, these projections affect our relationship to goals and connection with others. Understanding how projection is a major factor in every moment of our experience is essential to recognizing how our projections, clear or distorted, are serving or hurting us in our life.

Discerning projection requires the acknowledgment of self-power and self-responsibility in the ways and means of our role in the outcomes of our personal story. Revealing one's beliefs about the identity of self, the ideals for self, and how these two aspects are being applied and operated from is the first step to discerning how one affects their life, manifesting conflict or harmony that rules each experience. Balance and compassion are essential to aligning the identity of self and the ideal of self, as one projects their thoughts, emotions, beliefs, and choices in the world. Distortion and perceived failures arise from lack of awareness or the imbalance of one's beliefs about identity and what they actualize in the world that is unclaimed or disowned as "not self" when the source is rooted from within. If one denies the opportunity to sort out the resistance within and acts without awareness of self, any face from the maze of mirrors has the opportunity to project. Most often, imprinted paths of response based on previous experiences will dominate one's projections in circumstance. These templates become malleable through introspection and awareness that allow one to define new structures of response. Then one may be compelled to act differently in the evolution of self-identity and empowered accountability for the narrative of one's life.

As one cultivates greater awareness of self-identity, expectations of self and others, and programmed responses that influence perceptions and actions at each stage of one's journey, the potency of intention and empowered humility has the opportunity to build a healthy skill in the manifestation of experiences. This understanding supports the psyche's process of releasing karmic debt prior to the walk of the soul through death, enabling peace, resolve, and appreciation to lighten one's steps during the experience of living. Acknowledging that reaching clarity beyond distortion is a practice everyday is a step toward releasing resistance. This inspires continued effort for aligning one's perceptions of self in the world to one's ideals of self in the world.

All relationships with other individuals in life increase the demand for clarifying projections of self and projections of others. The closer one is to other individuals, the more pressure one may feel in the exchange of ideas, feelings, beliefs, and therefore choices. Discerning projection is imperative for strength and liberation when enduring conflict and embracing the invitation of co-creation as one commits to the exploration of manifesting fulfilling outcomes for more than self. When applying ones understanding of self-projection and the perceived projections of others, greater skill in communication can be derived. This requires patience, compassion, devotion, and forgiveness for the process of evolution we are each influenced by. It is important to break bad habits of assumption by remembering to be curious of the why and how of our own perceptions and the perceptions of others. Every individual has a different maze of mirrors to work with and different capacities for introspection, sorting, and organizing awareness of self and others. Choosing discernment instead of judgment and refining one's filter for how one receives and responds confirms integrity with accountability for self. This allows one to honor the needs for self in an empowered way that does not seek to dominate the process of others.

Projections are a part of self, others, and "the world as we know it." Projection can lead us deep into a maze of self where confusion and despair take over and it can lead us out of the maze with clear intention to manifest one's evolving capacity for fulfillment with self and with others in community. Other helpful tools for refining projections include journaling, reflecting, affirmations, and mantras. Awareness of how one aligns and applies the balance of the perceived self and the actualized self, offers expandable skills in strategizing how and what one manifests. Re-tuning one's filter of projections can support the release and transmutation of limiting beliefs such as judgment, victimization, disparity consciousness, and the experience of suffering perceived through one's lifetime. Self-limiting beliefs that create more resistance and more suffering are a hallmark of the maze of mirrors. The way through the maze is through re-orienting to a state of mind that encourages curiosity and learning. One that allows for win-win and win or learn perceptions of experience for better future outcomes. This is how one rewrites the patterns of their own personal narrative.

~Empower the narrative perceived by discerning projection's seed. Refine the programs within to manifest from clarity and cultivate the skill to co-create responsibly.~

IV

❦

Discerning Projection and Healthy Communication

Communication is the cornerstone of human consciousness that stabilizes expansion and growth into other aspects of awareness that open the door to what and how we manifest as individuals and as a collective. Communication with self and communication with others to enable opportunities for success in our endeavors is essential in the awareness of each moment. Projection of one's thoughts and feelings in every context of experience is imperative for healthy communication. Discernment of how these projections affect self and others requires curiosity in the awareness of self and others.

Healthy communication is founded in efforts that seek clarity, openness to working with differing or opposing perceptions, and intentions for positive outcomes. This requires compassion for self and compassion for others in the active process of discerning projection. We are all on a path to understanding what it is to be human, how to push the limits of our perceptions, and the cultivation of the many evolving dimensions of consciousness. Discernment is different than judgment when assessing thoughts and feelings. Discernment is an objective acceptance of context, factors, and personal conclusions that releases the concept of right versus wrong and the impulse to blame, shame, guilt, or condemn that judgment asserts. From a place of discernment one can more accurately assess belief patterns in self or others and how they function to create harmonic or dissonant outcomes.

Harnessing one's awareness of projection from old belief patterns, experiential imprints, passionate ideals, and hidden desires is the key to acting in every moment with accountability and adaptability. When projections are clarified as an active element in each context one's precision for successful outcomes is substantially strengthened. Even if the outcome of a circumstance is not what we intended or desired, the knowledge of self and how to orient oneself based on the discernment of projections of self or others and the effort of healthy communication enacted is alchemical gold. Every experience no matter the suffering carries its pearl. This pearl teaches us there is always light within darkness, a seed of beauty in the mundane, an ember of gratitude beneath grief, and a chapter of wisdom in the book of growth beyond surviving.

Human beings have proven over the ages on earth their persistence to create, harness resources, and establish complex structures of communication to enlarge and expand the concepts of civilization. Much of this productivity has been directed outside the self with a gradual deepening of internal awareness for the effect our actions have on self, mentally and emotionally, connections with others, and the environment we co-exist in. In the 20th century much of the modern world accomplishments have enabled and stimulated introspection of the individual beyond concerns of the collective. With this shift has come greater challenges to discerning the increased projections that arise during the expansion of one's conscious awareness of self and eventually others. The mind is like a computer uploading and downloading files constantly. More RAM is required to sustain continued input and proper organization of that input. Introspection is like defragmenting the files of one's software and upgrading the capacity to function with higher efficiency. Actively choosing to assess oneself and assess others in any context with the tools of discernment, accountability, and adaptability fortifies the efficiency and endurance of healthy communication.

Projection starts within as one filters their experiences with the world personally and impersonally. Acknowledging self from not self is the first step to clarification for potential sovereignty from the effect of other's thoughts, emotions, and actions. The second step is reflecting in how one's own thoughts, emotions, and actions are serving or blocking the outcomes in life and one's personal story. Distinguishing ideals vs. realistic factors and abilities in the present context is key for directing one's intention to align their thoughts, feelings, and actions with the most harmonious outcomes for their personal story. Once this alignment has been tended, attention to the personal and impersonal response one has to other's beliefs, thoughts, emotions, and actions can be concluded. From this base of understanding communication styles, compassionate wording, respect for others voice, and receptivity to co-creative reflection that expands ones understanding in a healthy way may be applied. Healthy communication is the bridge to opportunities for healing, holistic conclusion, growth, and forward progress through unity with others or the freedom of an individual from lingering conflict with self or others.

Discernment of projection applied to self, others, and the effect on circumstances is a tool that bestows greater potency and versatility when conflict arises in self or with others. Once developed, clarity in the origin of oneself and the effect thoughts, emotions, and actions have in one's life narrative cultivates energy conservation, restoring the mind and heart from the incessant drain of unresolved experiences. Healthy communication, with self and with others, utilizing the awareness of projection in a compassionate way, further empowers the connection with self and the connection with others collectively. We are all acting from a maze of mirrors. The way we project these perceptions and filter information received externally or inspired within is in direct relationship to the conscious or unconscious actions and intentions that effect the outcomes of circumstance, including the degree of suffering and success one perceives.

~Be curious. Embrace the pearl in every moment. Harness discernment to lead with intention and accountability in the narrative you create. Engage the alchemy of self and expand your capacity for wholeness.~

V

The Relationship Between Confidence and Motivation

Confidence and motivation are essential components of progress for the self and for community. The dynamic use of creativity with confidence and motivation to achieve a goal expands the opportunities one has in life and shares with others. The motivation for introspection combined with the confidence one holds in their personal perceptions and capabilities, directly relates to the sense of motivation and confidence one feels when aspiring to achieve. It is the introspection, to deepen our awareness that is paramount in building the foundations of confidence and restoring the reservoir of motivation during times of ease and times of hardship. Confidence and motivation fuel one another inter-dependently, generating a sustained effectiveness to one's endeavors.

From childhood, the imprint of our experiences may nourish or impede the foundations of one's sense of confidence and motivation to aspire and achieve progressive goals or make effective choices that expand one's skills for success in life. These goals include acquiring basic needs for survival, personal desires in development and refinement of one's personality, and goals considered to be a contribution to others in the concentric circles of community. (In order, respectively.) If one does not achieve a healthy foundation of inner confidence and apply motivations to learn and succeed in the world, the supportive cycle of these two attributes for progress and fulfillment is distorted. The struggle to engage one is compounded by a lack in the other, yet the opportunity to harness these dynamic concepts is not lost. Acknowledging one's creative force of existence and the passion latent within, may still act as a spark for confidence or motivation and initiate the interdependent cycle of one to the other.

Every day, every failed endeavor, and every successful endeavor may be utilized as a doorway to invite the motivation within in order to refine one's strategies and to progress into something one aspires to. One must watch out for preconceived convictions and confirmation bias where the intent to demotivate or subdue confidence may be limiting. Seeking power beyond these detracting thought-forms, imprinted by previous experiences, requires openness to resetting that bias. Learning and revising strategy, after affirming attention and openness, is the next stage of learning how to access opportunities.

Opportunity is like a chariot carrying one toward the healthy perpetuation of confidence and motivation. When one does not see opportunity in its simple forms, one is blinded by bias to the existence of opportunity in other forms and other offerings. A keen eye may see a multitude of opportunities in one moment, while those who do not look at all cannot expect to see. The evidence of success with contentment and ambition, rooted in diligence to continue endeavoring new goals in life and in our awareness of self, is directly relevant to the strength of one's confidence and motivation.

No matter the false starts, failures, extensive abundance, or tides of gains and losses, every individual has the choice, the power of life, to tap into a spark of motivation. In order to develop the perception of fulfillment through earning success, in all applicable senses, an individual must feel the achievement of goals. These goals may be small and quantitative, initially, with the eventual expansion of larger goals based on grander qualitative differentiation. Either way, quantity and quality are a part of the equation when seeking the sum of fulfillment. They are a part of every choice and confidence is intricately woven into the fabric of one's perceptions through the evidence of achievement.

Knowing the strength of confidence and motivation within endows an expanding sense of autonomy. Autonomy is a gift we grant ourselves through successive development, harvested in our endeavors. This sense of autonomy is evident in the innovations and inventions of humankind. Yet, the potency of autonomy may create attitudes of severe independence and a disconnection from the resources and factors required in our experience of cultivating autonomy. Maintaining the integrity of self-awareness and one's effect on others in society and the natural world beyond is essential to sustaining the co-creative relationship of existence. Releasing excessive feelings of control and self-righteousness is imperative to the perpetuation of qualitative confidence and motivation, founded in the awareness that life is not about "us" only. Life is not about your family only, humankind only, or the earth only.

Life is about all things existing in the physical world and all perceptions, thought or felt, in the intangible world that is inside each of us. Likewise, achievement and success are not about individual choice, alone. Nor are they about one choice, itself. They require many elements and many choices along the path of one's experiences. As a community, we have the power to make many choices together in the opportunities that arise. How confident we are in the understanding of our perceptions and actions in life and how motivated we are to work together to achieve group endeavors is a direct reflection of the inherent sense of autonomy in every individual.

~Tides of success and failure flow in and out of individual lives and societies, as a whole. The opportunity to progress is ignited by intentional motivation and empowered by the healthy confidence in our will to achieve. It is a perpetual rhythm in the breath of existence to aspire and endeavor. ~

VI

⚜

Creativity and Self-Care

As we navigate the world and everyday routines, the call for more energy to feed the machine is continuous. Each designated "to do" or spontaneous agreement to fulfill the space of time requests that we initiate and express our vitality to meet the demand. How often do we stop and check in with our capacity to meet those demands? Like feeding gas to the vehicles that so often cart us around and money to the bank for the amenities we require, the tank of our vitality must be refilled.

Sleep brings restoration for some and appeases the want for stillness in the mind but does it really fill the zephyr of our vitality? Does it inspire and engage us to feel the dynamic sense of desire within to carry out our routines and stated commitments for work and play? The act of creating energy requires all aspects of our body, heart, mind, and spirit be present and contributing. Creating energy also requests a call to unity in all of these aspects of our being, in order to fully embrace the experience of life. Understanding how to recycle, restore, and recreate energy is equally essential for the perception of wholeness and contentment about one's life. This awareness goes beyond the basics of food, sleep, sex, and general physical health.

In our deep biological well our need to create and externalize from within resonates evidently in the world around us. The higher mind transforms the possibilities for manifestation beyond this base urge and many opportunities to explore how and what we create are born. Innovations, inventions, positive community exchange, opportunities to reflect, and physical exercise all have a cyclical relationship to our "creative manifest" and restoration of self. Art and time in nature offer us a higher degree of simplicity and restoration. If we immerse ourselves in the experience of nature and creating art, the balance of return is most often greater than the expenditure. Even if we participate in these acts with an array of emotion, there is a still point and a quieting they both offer in service of the heart, mind, and spirit. This is where the zephyr and inspiration are instilled, expanded, and perpetuated.

Even if one feels they are not "creative" the opportunity to access this with increased opening to awareness and practice exists. Creating art is about the freedom "to be"; just as our immersion in nature, in a sanctuary of our choosing, is as well. Art can be the primer for deep reflections and conclusions. It can be a release point for what we seek to express or let go of; to move energy with intent out of our body. Art for the sake of art, whether to keep or throw away, is a powerful potentiator for that sense of fulfillment one may feel is just out of their reach.

Over the years my art has taken on many forms and I have observed many subject matter for my expression of experience. I have explored archival and degenerative art for their different purposes and I have changed my style again and again until feeling fully connected to a style that is most authentic to the language I speak. Through my various forms of expression, painting has always been a mainstay, but I feel the acknowledgment and intention of art has its place in everything. From house projects to camping spots, cooking to decorating; art is life. For me, that means creativity may be intentionally strategic or fun and freeing. This definition changes, depending on the person/artist and each state of beingness.

Moving my paintbrush along the path of an object to define it with a mix of stochastic feathering and dabbing, in order to depict the play of shades and colors in the formless, is a language. The way we speak, the way we move, are languages of expression that reveal a story, an intention, and a persona. Physical movement with freedom and exploration is another profound form of art, embodied. It is another prime example of a fulfilling method that builds energy for release and restoration of the creative flow, reconsolidating the vitality within. Dancing and explorative movement may be the most tangible form of art and creativity within because it puts us in our core and requires the full attention of mind and body to channel the heart and soul.

"Get out of the box", we say. Move beyond the confining rules of routine and conserving one's thoughts, feelings, and actions. Channel it in that sacred moment with self in nature or making art. Art does not need to be defined as one way or with one medium. There is an abundance of forms in art to be witnessed and learned from until one discovers what works best for them. Let the pressure of projections to see what you create as "perfect" or exact fall away and remember art is like life. It is a process, a give and take, for experience. How much control one seeks will change the perception of fulfillment to be instilled.

~Recall the inner child when new experiences were just fun and exploratory. This is the origin of the higher mind and spirit, creating in our world with enthusiasm. That enthusiasm engages a reflective and inspiring cycle that paradoxically fulfills while initiating a flow through the process of achieving that awareness perpetually. Access the essential urge and flow into the heArt of wonder.~

VII

❧

How Fear and Love affect Free Will

Free will is a foundational attribute of all higher order beings in the animal kingdom. The resonance of consciousness paired with mobile limbs creates an opportunity to choose how to direct our abilities physically in the needs for survival and the desires of the heart and mind. The instinctual duality of fear and love is innate to the processes of our interpretations and reactions to the world. These interpretations program our responses to the world as safe or unsafe and nourishing or detrimental. These programs reflect in the perceptions of our choices as effective or ineffective. Free will is the wild card we carry in the face of any fatalistic belief or experience that incites a feeling of powerlessness. Free will is what makes us autonomous in our hearts and minds, no matter the circumstances of our physical being. To disregard one's free will is to become a slave or a martyr to an experience, a person, or a society.

The concept of being born free has merit no matter your race, country of origin, or childhood narrative. The concepts of fear and love within one's perceptions of the world are what hold the power to confine and disregard free will or to activate and pursue it. All the layers of experience one records from the youngest age, along with climactic moments of reckoning, throughout life, create structures of belief. These beliefs define ones' capacity to make choices and shift the paradigm of ones' foundation. Honoring sovereignty by harnessing free will motivates one to envision and embrace new opportunities for success.

Fear is a basic instinct, yet in the mind it may be cultivated as an irrational response. Once the analysis of an experience is rationalized, the persistent cycling of a rationale can cause the perception of fear to assert itself in circumstances that are irrelevant to the initial association of fear. If one sees the world through a lens of fear it is a natural reflex to contract away or to destroy the triggering factor in order to "get away." If this perception and behavior perpetuates, it will result in strict limitations on the observance and enactment of one's own free will. Being open to an experience or shutting down to an experience are the most basic responses we have in life. The more we shutdown from experience due to fear, the more we enslave and martyr ourselves to our perceived limitations. The more we open to experience and learn how to navigate our use of free will in choice, the more we expand our perceived limitations and allow the possibilities of what we seek and welcome in to succeed.

In the mind, each hemisphere represents this duality of possibility. When cultivated, both offer the tools to be more conscientious in order to change our world, beginning with our choices and the narrative we live by. The left hemisphere is calculating, coordinating, and structuring. The right hemisphere is imaginative, "sensory feelingness", and abstract in its' associative processing. Both are required for holistic interpretation and meaning. Both are required in the act of free will and the choice to redefine meaning and importance in our perceptions.

In brain development and evolution, the reptilian hindbrain or brainstem coordinates all the basic functions of survival. It communicates with memory banks to associate fear driven responses. The mammalian brain or limbic system associates the experiences of connection, sensuality, and emotional impulses. These developmental imprints cultivate family dynamics and social interactions as another aspect of survival that expands the capacity of our species to create together. The prefrontal lobes and cortex, also called the executive brain, is evolving currently and interconnecting many pathways for consciousness and self-awareness. This aspect of the brain enables one to separate the imprinted patterns and base functions of the mammalian (love compelled) and reptilian (fear driven) brain regions. The executive brain increases the capacity for choice and free will through understanding how our drives and perceptions of self benefit or challenge us. Here we carry the key to unlocking the greatest powers of the mind that are innate to our genome, as well as the keys to directing the expansion of our evolution as conscious beings beyond what we know of ourselves.

The initial drive of the will is to survive. The secondary impulse of the will is to connect with others and nourish oneself with pleasure and contentment. The tertiary invitation of will is to define and design experiences that bring wonder, mindfulness, and the expansion of perception and communication in order to act with intention. Accessing and utilizing the power of the mind beyond inherent drives and impulses requires responsibility and account-ability. It is essential to weigh the balance of how programmed needs and wants are influencing our sense of free will. Our choices define the narrative we perceive as our life. If one responds with fear most often, the reactionary choices depict a life of many struggles with the sense of aloneness, based in survival mode. This brain loop can perpetuate after one or multiple traumatic experiences or from the perception of challenges in life we feel "are dealt to us." The "dealt to us" perception is a thin line. It can inspire us to work harder to enact free will or push us into beliefs of helpless victimization or ineffectual apathy.

If one responds with love most often, the responsive choice can portray a life of vulnerability mixed with feelings of appreciation, connection and support with others. A sense of struggle, being taken advantage of, and rejection can also result from an imbalance in how we navigate vulnerability. The truth about vulnerability is that it is inevitable. Whether one is fighting for survival in the physical or mental arenas or struggling for connection, identification, and the reciprocation of love from others, vulnerability is a perception of the executive mind as it begins to sort out the balance of needs and wants. Discovering and aligning a healthy balance in how love and fear inform us, creates greater opportunity to form structures of mindfulness and understanding in the experience of one's personal narrative. This power of awareness and choice opens the doorway to evolving the capacity of our species and our interactions in the world we inhabit. The power of free will succeeds when applied to how one recognizes and responds to internal beliefs and events in the external world.

The power of free will exists in the depths of our understand-ing that experiences are perceived and influenced by imprinted programs. These subconscious programs compel us to react with fear or respond with love. By choosing love and compassion for others or ourselves, the opportunities for fulfillment in life, beyond the challenges to connect and the battles to survive become inherent in the design of the experiences we define our life to be about. If you are here to have an experience of your own free will, how do you want your free will to serve you? Are you wired for fear or are you wired for love? How can you refine the balance of the way love and fear are informing you?

Conscious awareness of the biological and perceptual components of how one enacts their will, in each circumstance, is essential to harnessing the potency of one's free will. There are many faces of individual will including but not limited to, the will within to endure and overcome, the will within to suffer and resist, the will within to open, receive and share oneself, the will within to create as an individual and in community, and the will within to heal from internal and external conflict by refining the perceptions we carry about life and self. Even the choice to surrender is a willful act.

~Surrender to the journey of life and cultivate trust in your own free will. Seek the potency of an open heart beyond fear and embrace the keys within to redefine the limits of your perceived path.~

VIII

Consumption: Guilt, Resentment, and Regret

The energy in life required for fulfilling one's endeavors and maintaining innovative solutions for challenges that arise can be stifled by thought and emotion. These emotions and thoughts can create resistance to motivation and to clarity if left unidentified and unresolved. In a world that bases its' conditional beliefs on right versus wrong, the experiences of guilt, resentment, and regret are frequent. The opportunity to process perceptions and re-align one's understanding to release the drain of these foundational beliefs, in order to influence growth with liberating wisdom, is often lacking. The path of growth and liberation requires the application of compassionate communication with self and with others. Guilt, resentment, and regret are negative forms of reinforcement in the mind. They take more than they offer when viewed from a map of possibility in skill development, that engages motivation instead of inertia. While these negative re-enforcers do have the power to promote a sense of empathy for others and conscientiousness of self for one's role or effect in an experience, positive re-enforcers such as seeking understanding, acts of forgiveness, and harmonic resolutions for future similar contexts open the mind and heart to be inspired for different outcomes.

Inspiration naturally invokes a sense of vitality to engage with life, connection with one's endeavors, and with others. Guilt, resentment, and regret imprison the power of motivation and decrease one's self-esteem when it comes to capability, living forward beyond loss, and a healthy balance of accountability with self and others. Guilt, resentment, and regret all originate from the "Judge and Victim" narrative that superimposes itself on an individual's sense of willpower. This is not compassionate communication, which seeks understanding and authenticity of one's intention, without blame or shame, and consults a path to resolution that is chosen with the goal of mutual empowerment. Mutual empowerment enables inspiration to move beyond inertia and to motivate one's will to choose differently for more fulfilling outcomes.

The perception of one's "quality of life" can shift dramatically depending on the view of self as a part of this life. When one feels less capable, less effort is generated in the will to progress or even maintaining life at all. Depression and outrage are common digressions for depleted inspiration, self- esteem, and the will to learn. These digressions are a red flag that our emotions and thoughts imprinted by the experience of "Judge and Victim" roles have welded a sense of entrapment one is resigned to or rebelling against. To resolve depression and outrage, one must seek a new template for perceptual deduction that aligns with the liberation of the "Victim" within and reframes the "Judge" mentality to the role of a "Compassionate Guide." Active refinement of language in how one speaks to themselves is the first step to offering a more compassionate language with others. Examples may be similar to the following:

Judge: "Why are you always messing things up?"
Guide: "What is it that you cannot give yourself? Do you feel worthy?"

Judge: "Why do you have to react like that?"
Guide: "Why did you react? Does your reaction fit the moment? How can you respond instead of react?"

Judge: "You deserve this." "I don't deserve this."
Guide: "Based on your intention, do you deserve this? How can you learn from this outcome? Can you change it now or in the future to have a different, more fulfilling or appeasing outcome for all involved?"

In cultures and families across the world there are varying degrees of unhealthy reinforcement. The age of the individual, family fracturing, and institutional impressions have influenced a learning environment that calls for striving beyond the dissonance in order to achieve the feeling of wholeness in one's mind, heart, and spirit. This call to strive beyond signifies the potential of hierarchical brain development. Humans have been evolving greater use of the prefrontal lobes portion of the brain that have the capacity to shift the focus of the mind to learn vicariously, refine the process of understanding, and to create and choose differently. This means that healing imprints, learned from experiential awareness throughout one's life, is possible and may be used as a tool to purge the binds of guilt, resentment, and regret, or any other stuck emotions one suffers from. In the Patanjali Sutras, a sage is quoted as saying, "*The pain is inevitable the suffering is an option.*" Quality of life is sustained and expanded by one's capacity to grasp the teachings and allow thoughts and emotions to inform, from a place of guidance and curiosity, to create more successful outcomes instead of the confining judgments that demand consequential suffering from oneself or others.

The "Compassionate Guide" within may be likened to a merciful god or to a loving parent capable of being fully present as an extension of oneself. Even if the belief in a god or the existence of this benevolent parent is not a part of one's narrative, the desire for this loving embrace and guidance exists in each of us because the "inner child" still lives on as a part of the subconscious self. Guilt is a punishment to the inner child creating a victim experience by self or others and leaves a stigma until resolved. If guilt is left unresolved the stigma deepens, carving out a sense of self-doubt that mires healthy confidence. Resentment is consuming of one's life force, muddles mental emotional clarity, and blocks the path to resolution and closure. When resentment lingers unresolved, it begins to shut down the function of resourceful innovation and creativity, resulting in inertia. This inertia may affect many elements in one's life endeavors. Regrets are the empty shells of unresolved emotion that lack fulfillment in choices made or never embarked upon. The residue of regret can immerse one so deeply that vitality withers and motivation for dreaming forward fades. Regret is a stalemate in the mind that reveals the outcome of an inner conflict that has been given the power to rule one's life and perceptions of self, limiting the experience of self-acknowledgment and gratitude for what one has fulfilled. The more regrets, the less fulfilled one has allowed their self to be.

The re-enforcers that weaken one's ability to preserve vitality, inspiration for fulfillment, and quality of life may be consuming to the point of manifesting disease in the physical body. As vitality wanes in the presence of parasitic emotions and regeneration of inspiration for life endeavors reduces, the body follows suit with the mental emotional directive. In order to perpetuate one's potency of will and openness to life through learning and connection, attention to how one communicates with self and others is essential. When the perceptions of guilt, resentment, and regret arise, the act of choosing to be curious, to understand oneself and others, and to seek liberation through wisdom for creative solutions will lead the way to new paradigms. These new paradigms of thought, emotion, and creative choices, beyond judgment and victimization, override the programs that result in the experiences of suffering and inertia.

~Embrace your inner child with loving guidance and release limitations binding vitality. Choose compassionate forgiveness to allow receptivity for creative resolve. Seek a quality of life that inspires gratitude and embodies no regrets. ~

IX

The Faces of Humility

What is humility? Many religious texts and dictionaries define it as modesty or a lowly view of oneself. It may be applied to many moments as a state of humbleness, being grateful, for what you are given by others or the world and not being bold in asking for more than this. In the application of this base definition to everyday life little room is left for ambition and creativity that are the spark of one's personal power to have choices in each moment as we navigate life and to grow in the capacity for self-empowering abilities. Is humility really about being insignificant and humble? How far can we go in life believing this about ourselves and being dependent on others to give us what they think we should get or need? How does this work if we all live in this state of humbleness without a sense of shared power?

Psychoanalysis of the concept "humility" suggests that a well-rounded personality has a "healthy dose" of it, but what does that mean when applying the act of humility in worldly affairs and everyday circumstances? Does it mean settling for having the most basic "something", a job, a relationship, a lifestyle, in order to have them at all? Does it mean being quiet and accepting the abuse of others or having no voice when conflict and discontent arise? The balance of power is a teaching for the self in all aspects of life. Humility is one aspect of keeping that power in check. If that is the foundational purpose of humility, then a healthier interpretation may be refined.

Empowered humility is the awareness of one's own power within and the capacity to respond to any aspect of life. The cultivation of strength and temperance supports successful outcomes that align self with a shared sense of power in creation. This face of humility invites one to consider creative solutions that benefit self and others without the need for submission or dominion. Empowering oneself to achieve a sense of purpose in each endeavor of the life we lead encourages the manifestation of growth through learning how to wield and share our power with others. Empowering others through recognition and allowing the opportunity for shared endeavors and therefore outcomes is an act of applied humility. In this way we do not rely on others to give us power nor do we hold power over anyone else.

Empowered humility engages us to listen to what we are not hearing when a situation is not working the way we idealized. It calms the cycling of the mind when one's focus is only on the power loss or power gain of a conflict that arises. Receptivity is an extension in the awareness state of humility. When one is receptive, objectively and subjectively, one can be empowered with clarity and create opportunity for shared power. Attention to self is key for accountability and assessing how we could approach conflict differently to have more productive outcomes.

Accountability requires humility and attention to self as a factor in the circumstances we experience. Balanced self-empowerment for creative solutions that support shared power inspires deeper connection with one's personal sense of integrity and enables others to have the same empowerment for their own integrity. This establishes healthy foundations for the integrity of the connection itself, whether it's the connection of self to a desired achievement, a project with others, or the pursuit of sustainable relationships with family, friends, and lovers.

Another face of empowered humility acts as a balance to the success we perceive in the moment and life as a whole. With this awareness we can honor our choices and efforts for the achievements and abundance earned, while also acknowledging the help of others and the supportive factors that empowered one to fully succeed. Through awareness of our successes in this way compassion is cultivated to share power with others by acting in some way to guide or support them physically, mentally, and/or emotionally if they are open to receive. It is essential to understanding that sometimes what one has to offer out of the desire to share power is not being requested or openly received by others or situations we seek to give it to.

The attention to empowered humility returns that potency to self and invites us to release a sense of requirement to share power, thus restoring the balance of overexertion that enables the sense of struggle around power loss or power gain. Compassion for self is the graceful way to restore balance when one's call to give is excessive, unsustainable, and disempowering. Consistently applying empowered humility fortifies one's integrity with self and cultivates strategies to manifest success in our endeavors throughout the journey of life. When a power struggle results one can be sure that the skill of empowered humility, once harnessed, will protect against the loss of self-potency and sustain opportunities to manifest diplomatic and co-creative outcomes.

~Trust in the power of self and embody the skill of temperance to liberate oneself from the extremes of submission and dominion.~

X

❦

Devotion in Love

Devotion is loving dedication. Honest, intentional, realistic devotion maintains the intent to support one another in the context of a changing world and a changing relationship within that world. The old adage "Nothing stays the same" is directly relevant to any individual who holds sacred the ideology that devotion in love means your agreements and roles are only and forever the same as when you entered the agreement. Devotion in love as an agreement is not binding because devotion is something you create and re-create through exchange with yourself and with someone else. Devotion to self is as important in a relationship as one's devotion to another and for the relationship.

To offer loving support, encouragement, or celebration of another is a code of devotion. This offering brings honor and value to the path every individual is working out and deciding upon in their progression through life and the transformation of death. Unconditional love and support are consistent when the acceptance that the one supporting the other is not in control of that person's choices or the outcomes from those choices. It also offers the kind of support that comes without demand or control of the other person to be or choose what another wants, of and for them. The place where this conditionality is most easily witnessed is in the closest relationships one shares. Partners, children, lovers, family, and best friends, in this order respectively, each create an opportunity to assess and apply one's principles of conditional and unconditional love. It is human nature to subconsciously presume that these types of relationships are extensions of ourselves or dictate our thoughts and actions around principles for how we perceive connection, life, and death. The cause and effect of conditional love is that it begets more conditional love. The question remains: Does conditional love create true respect and devotion for another or is it only the illusion of respect dictated by the framework of agreements that demand dedication and respect? How can one offer and receive respect without demanding or needing to control the agreement?

This is the point and offering of unconditional love. Embracing a code of love as a part of the exchange that honors what we witness in others and supports them by communicating effectively through problem solving to reach mutual decisions for a relationship creates natural appreciation and builds respect. Effective communication that expands consideration of choices for others without attachment to it being "our way" advocates the inspiration and re-creation of devotion. This approach contrasts greatly in the long-term struggles of identity and mutuality in relationship. It is the difference between demanding dedication and controlling the agreement with inviting devotion and sharing the merit of each other's experiential desires.

To be clear, conditional love is not a bad thing, nor is conditional or unconditional love a single choice in how to practice love. Conditional love is an essential part of understanding one's personal needs and wants and perceiving to what extent others are capable of meeting those demands. Conditional love creates protective boundaries from certain undesired experiences that unconditional love does not. Yet, unconditional love is the seed of one's deepest desires to be valued beyond all reason. It is the foundation of perpetuating connection with others so that we are not alone or pushed to the "me against the world" cynicism that is devoid of feeling loved and valued by others. Unconditional love provides a doorway in our confined experiences of the analytical machine we call "mind". It softens the fortress one builds around oneself as they create more and more conditions throughout life, upon themselves, and others. This doorway is the one we as children walk through and children remind us of. Unconditional love is a natural experience until defined otherwise by perceptions in the mind. The perceptions one develops may block or create opportunity to refine solutions in the tidal flow of circumstances and how we manifest our ideals of connection in life.

Building a bridge in the concepts of conditional love that supports unconditional love for intentional fulfillment, is just as essential as applying unconditional love to support the modulation of applied conditions for healthy boundaries in lieu of a commanding fortress. The offering of unconditional love and the intentional awareness of how conditional love effects outcomes of devotion in love, over time, are essential to effective co-creation and perpetuation of devotion in every relationship.

~Devotional love is not given freely by demands and control. It is inspired by invitation and requests. Speak your intention with compassion and strengthen your voice for healthy boundary in dedication to open the mind and heart for sustainable co-creation.~

XI

❧

How We Connect & Define
a Sense of Loyalty

Humans love connection. Even the generalized introvert finds comfort in connection one on one with select individuals. Connection and sharing of oneself can be valued in different ways. Some prefer quiet physical presence, others mental processing and reflection. Some feel connection with emotional or spiritual identification and many feel connection in all of these ways equally.

Connectivity to another or a group of others in community brings us feelings of comfort, confidence, exaltation, and unity beyond separateness. Loyalty in each connection may look different based on the foundation and cultivation of connection in simplistic or complex forms. Some individuals live by strict codes of loyalty to self and others, while some have no code or flexible codes of loyalty based on their own degrees of life experience and mindfulness. Conflict arises between loyalty and the connectivity of individuals or individuals to society relevant to the lack of adherence to a mutually agreed upon code or differing codes and values for self and others.

Assuming that connection automates loyalty in the same definition in which we perceive the code of loyalty and expectations within ourselves is a mistake often made. Without communication and display through experience one cannot be certain the loyalty they offer others will be reciprocated, especially where the context of loyalty is to be applied. The roles we take on for the world and others have a strong influence in our sense of constancy and adherence to a code before we apply this to others in community. The depth of connection is unreliable to creating assumptions that values of loyalty are in agreement. Honest communication and outlining of our personal integrity with self, vocally and by demonstration, is the clearest way of preparing a basis for expectation. This fortifies our mindfulness of self and others seeking clarity about the foundation of the connection and its offerings. How embodied and reliable our power for bonding and loyalty is may only be edified by the constancy of our application through experiences with others over time. To make assumptions otherwise may bare the result of increased judgment and suffering that result in separation and loss of connection.

Throughout life, experiences will call on us to have greater loyalty to oneself, at times and at other times, a more fortified loyalty to others. Negative experiences with others or self –destructive tendencies will challenge our sense of loyalty and connection to everything and perhaps cause a full deconstruction or re-construction of one's sense of dedication in all respects. Discerning our value in each connection for its role in our lives dictates the degree and quantity of connections we acknowledge as meaningful. In the history of society, family blood has been primary in association of code with respect to deep connections and loyalty. Beyond this, partnership and groups of individuals with common rituals and beliefs sequentially align to test our values, capacity for exchange, and foundations of loyalty. In today's society, the break down of family structure, healthy relationship, and codes of expectation have shifted the reliance and alliance onto self and partnership, first and foremost, or to community groups with a common purpose. The lack of historical life experience and cultivation of code in developmental years has extended the time it takes to attain deep bonds of trust in the loyalty of others. Yet, in our idealism or jadedness, assumptions are still often made.

Without mindfulness and open communication emotions of betrayal and desire for more than others display often take the lead in the fall out of expectations unmet. Conflictive or degrading communication through blaming or avoidance and passive aggression may ensue. The way to satisfying connections with others is through healthy communication and mindfulness of self. The way to resolve conflict from assumptions and miscommunication is through assessing the desired outcome we seek; after the perceived value of that relationship has been made conscious. Then, strategizing ways to achieve that desirable outcome. Sometimes the most pertinent way is simply patience and inaction beyond judgment. Acknowledging that it may be most important for the other in relationship to be focused in connection and loyalty to their own needs for a period of time is a compassionate offering that may fortify the depth of the shared connection itself.

Discernment of how to proceed in resolving inner conflict over the feelings of separateness or a failure to meet expectations by other(s) requires a review of one's personal code. This includes the code of loyalty, compassionate connection for self and other, and one's capacity to embrace the different seasons of life the timeline of connection to others brings. The most harmonious and creative way to approach the foundational development and phases of reconstruction in our values of connection and loyalty is to lead by example in our dedication to a clear code. Communicating this to oneself and others in the face of fresh or established expectation is essential. Mindfulness of assumptions we make and assessment of expectations others state or enact by application to us is imperative to the clarity of an operable code connection is founded in. The persistence of values may be maintained as each individual aligns through shared experiences, cultivating a sense of unity and the power to create together for longevity.

When challenges and change arise, the strength of integrity in the code of connection acts like a pillar of stability to secure one's emotional, mental, and spiritual states during the process of transformation. The offering of stability and connection is a sacred gift in the many storms life brings. The experience of unity beyond separateness, trust, and doubt may be the primary elements that fortify the survival of individual potency, thus humanity, and the alchemy of soul.

~Unveil the cords that connect you to others. Authenticate the path of integrity with self. Unify the perceptions of mind and heart to empower actions that manifest the harmonic wisdom conceived in every fertile moment.~

XII

⟨❦⟩

When Self-Entitlement Becomes Self-Sabotage

In the current age of consciousness, attitudes of self-entitlement for the sake of identity acknowledgment and a wide definition of what it means to be privileged are common topics for discussion or conflict for division. The term self-entitlement may be defined as someone's personal assessment of what they feel they deserve in any context or circumstance. Self-entitlement arises in a world of duality where the balance of extremes is increasingly polarized. This context of polarization may be based in factual reality or rationalized perceptions. It is essential in the integrity of one's efforts for self-empowerment, in any context, to achieve a balance between personal perceptions, the perceptions of others, and factual reality.

When one's perception of self and focus on entitlement is the only catalyst, self-sabotage is more likely to prevail and ongoing conflict in self, the world, and relationships to what we seek to attain will perpetuate. Self-sabotage is a prominent cause of many unfulfilled endeavors in life. How aware an individual is of the components that drive their perceptions and actions or that compel their wants and needs will affect the success or failure in achieving resolve and fulfillment. These base factors, occurring in a situation or person beyond one's self focus, require acknowledgment and fine tuned clarity to affect intentional outcomes as well.

Self-sabotage may arise as harsh judgments of self or others, a lack of awareness of the integral parts to achieving an endeavor, or a fixation on perceived wants and needs that create a block to healthy communication with self and others. Self-sabotage is a representation of loss and brings the cathartic stages of grief into our being to be processed. Anytime an individual impedes the creative flow to seek or create solutions to a conflict, the compartmentalization required to ignore the conflict or the grief that results from it, fragments the mind, heart, and soul. Years later, these wounds manifest physically and mentally as stuck forms of guilt, resentment, and regret, degrading further the connections to the identity of self. If the goal of self-entitlement is to be acknowledged and given the wants or needs for the identity of self, one feels most aligned with, it is essential that self-sabotaging thoughts and actions be sorted and overcome.

Self-sabotage itself perpetuates the experience of self-entitlement due to the experiential conflict in a lack of fulfillment. This conflict may pivot one deeper into obstinacy for what they feel "owed" or toward an attitude of defeat with decreasing self-worth. This downward spiral of belief in "not deserving" something is the other side of failing to achieve wants, needs, and self-empowering opportunities for conflict resolution. It is imperative when one is fixated on perceptions of self-entitlement that a weighing of value in the whole circumstance, the whole life picture, and the origins of "why" one is entitled are clear. Understanding this opens a path to consider "how" this can be fulfilled or if it is, in fact, a fixation that may lead to sabotage.

Projections of belief around right versus wrong and declarations of identity in the context of day to day circumstance or larger social movements are a common driver of conflict and division in America and the world society. The identity of younger generations mixing with older generations will always bring pressure to re-define established institutions and the status quo of many topics. How we as conscious beings choose to create or offer healthy communication around these differences will be evident in the degree of divisiveness and outward display of power that result from self-entitlement. Will the enactments of perceived needs and wants be productive or sabotage the ideal sought for fulfillment? The path to weaving a fabric of ideas with foundational wisdom, fundamental facts, aspiring visions, and stable restructuring for refinement in the progression of humanity as a society on the earth require an eye for detail and openness to learning more than we think we know. Putting the microscope to self, others, the relationships shared, and the context of circumstance to expand one's perspective of all the multidimensional factors in an experience is the most empowering approach for self-fulfillment and attaining successful outcomes beyond self-entitlement and sabotage.

The terms self-entitlement and self-sabotage resonate with subjectivity and emotion revealing their enactment is primarily based on internal perceptions and conflicts with self. To use these terms, may automatically disregard all others in the context of an experience and shut down the creative flow of communication that may enable mutual empowerment and fulfillment. When working through a conflict of perception or need, refining terms for healthy communication may include phrases regarding "personal values", "personal boundaries for requirement", "definitions of integrity for self", "personal ideals" and "personal doubts", "inner conflict", "awareness of blocks in personal choices", and "accountability for reactivity", respectively.

It takes effort and commitment to consider the many factors affecting perceptions and outcomes for self and the world in this journey of life. Emotional reactivity without questioning one's impulses is a "trial and error" way of living that sets up more circumstances relating to cyclical patterns of self-sabotage and the sabotage of others, feeding conflict and separatism. Emotions are an informative element of what is calling for deeper introspection and sorting before enacting one's free will to choose with greater effectiveness for outcomes. Defaulting to impulsivity catalyzed by emotion in the fixation of self-entitlement or herd mentality without analysis for the value of the demand, the "why", and the "how to achieve" for optimal success, forfeits the most empowering aspect of choice in free will. Emotional attachments to what is valued in life vary with every individual. This subjective lens can polarize the simplest of moments dictated by the value systems one has created in their comparison of life experiences and outcomes.

Value systems are initiated in childhood and learned or taught by parental observation and dictation. Throughout life, the body, the heart and mind are only as mature as the challenges that have been influential in the growth of perceptions one has experienced. This includes perceptions of self-identity, others, the world, and self in context to all external factors. The superficiality and the profoundness of values may only be realized through the effort and commitment to analyzing and understanding the origins and drive behind expectations, wants, and needs. Assessing this information in the context of factual reality maintains a grounded perspective in the balance of fulfilling self and others. Expanding one's perception of value may be achieved by considering the lives and values of others.

In times of friction, the want for change is inevitable. Defining the terms for optimal resolve to empower and honor the integrity and inner wisdom of all involved requires effort and detailed awareness for healthy communication. Expanding the effectiveness of one's free will in choice demands discernment and an open mind for creative solutions beyond impulsive emotions and reactivity.

-Empower yourself without disempowering others. Weigh your expectations of yourself and the world. Seek the path where they connect and enable the opportunity for collective unity. Build a bridge between old and new structures of achievement to nourish integration for stable growth as each new day unfolds.-

XIII

❦

Compassionate Communication for Conflict Resolution

When conflict arises, how we handle it has everything to do with the outcome. Meeting conflict with intense reactivity only perpetuates the experience of dissonance, argumentation, and the pressure for divergence without resolve. An individual may resolve to avoid, discard, or defer the moment of conflict but this choice hardly ever leads to true resolution with clarity and closure about the experience in the heart and mind. Communication offers understanding, acknowledgment, and co-creative strategies for ultimate closure. Compassionate communication enables a healthy path to mediation of differences established with intention to clarifying, healing, and supporting all involved to seek mutual fulfillment in the outcome of an experience. This is applicable even if going separate ways or agreeing to disagree is a part of the outcome decision.

Common strategies to resolving conflict may include submitting, apologizing even when we feel its unnecessary, clarifying one's role in a disagreement and other's involved, shutting down and refusing to communicate, attacking other(s) in the disagreement repeatedly without acknowledging their feelings or thoughts, attempts to manipulate others to submit to us, and choosing attitudes of self-righteousness which polarize an individual's position further in an effort to defend oneself from receiving the beliefs or statements of another as credible. Strategies for compassionate communication include requesting time to consider the nature of the conflict, responding with acknowledgment for the experience of others in the disagreement, allowing more than one perception of a situation to have credibility, using tone and language in an openhearted, receptive, honoring, and intentional way to find harmony and release that serves all involved. In any attempt for resolution or experience of resistance it is imperative to acknowledge that each individual processes information differently and has their own blind spots when it comes to awareness of self, awareness of others, and awareness of the factors related to the nature of a conflict. When disagreement or resistance occurs which strategy do you often align with? Does the strategy change dependent on your orientation to a disagreement? Why is this the way you react or respond when dissonance happens?

Questioning the root of how one responds to conflict, resistance, and opportunities to consider the differences between others and self is key to understanding who you are and if you like who you are by witnessing those relative responses. Clarifying the origin of one's values and validating those values aside from the imprints and influences that may have caused one's attachment to those values is also a keystone to aligning with integrity and authenticity. Assessing how to modify one's approach to conflict with self and others in a compassionate way allows for quicker resolutions and holistic closure with transmutation of inflictions or projected imprints derived from moments of disharmony. With practice, frequency and intensity of conflicts will decrease and be evident in how an individual responds to resistance and disagreements. This is applicable to internal and external conflicts of the mind and heart in this experience of being human.

Being intentional with our words and meaning what we say to ourselves and to others is the path to greater harmony and creative solutions when misunderstanding, conflictive perceptions of a situation, differing values, and emotional intensity are present. The experience of anger, guilt, resentment, and regret sit heavily on the mind and heart, manifesting physically as ailments or disease. These undertones of thought and emotion are relevant in lack of closure and continual conflict. The ratio of conflict and holistic closure in one's life is a direct reflection of the strategies utilized to end resistance. Which is more important to you, the goal to win or the goal for peace? Compassionate communication originates and upholds the intention for both, for all involved. There is a balance between defining the differences and beliefs in oneself and with honoring the perceptions others upheld in themselves creating resistance. There is a balance in defending one's personal boundaries and accepting the needs and wants of others. There is not one authority, one truth, or one sense of right or wrong in a shared experience. Agreements are made with open communication and receptivity to the wisdom each carries to align with their most authentic self and to share that with others.

Willingness to learn through communication and have patience for every individual to process the opportunities to perceive something greater within self and utilize it to achieve healthier strategies for fulfillment in life is a gift to self and to others. Conflict may be painful in undefined or very evident ways but suffering beyond the pain of conflict is perpetuated because of poor strategies in communication, unwillingness to learn from experience, and a lack of resolve for healthy fulfillment.

~Seek the will to compassion when conflict arises. Harness the opportunity to heal and to grow for self and with others. Choose transmutation over suffering and learn to wield the staff of a mentor with the pen of a student. ~

XIV

❧

Being a Witness and Experiencing the Synchrony of Life

Through the course of life experience, we each take on the role of witnessing. A conscious mind in a vessel with senses to perceive endows our witnessing opportunities with tools that may be refined for discernment. What we discern or conclude may be simple or complex in its value and effect how we choose to apply those conclusions to new or similar circumstances. Being a witness of one's environment and of others is automatic and instinctual as we navigate basic drives to fulfill needs for survival and sustainability. Being a witness of self and how we interact with our environment and others is the next level of tool refinement, essential for expanding our experience as an individual that is part of a collective. The higher degrees of more practiced witnessing in all aspects begins to reveal a synchrony. This synchrony is relevant to one's discernment of the patterns inherent in the interactions of others and oneself, in the context of environmental factors.

Every moment is a multidimensional experience with different lenses of perception that shift in correlation to our objective and subjective states of awareness. Some people are wired to perceive the world with a subjective eye, while others embrace a more objective position. Being a witness of self creates an opportunity to learn how to be more of each. It takes a consistent receptivity for the journey into feeling and understanding all emotions, combined with analyzing and questioning our intentions, beliefs, fears, and desires with respect to outcomes. Acknowledging one's choices and accountability in our efforts or acquiescence about affecting the world around us is preliminary in the reflection of our conclusions about the patterns of synchrony to be witnessed.

Confirmation bias, conviction bias, and self-fulfilling prophecy are parts of the witnessing experience. That is why it is essential to break the habit of assumption and check in with the imprint of our reactions and urges. One must harness a sustained curiosity in the comparable differences and similarities of each experience. The question of reality or illusion can dictate projections we or others may assert to be accepted or rejected in each circumstance. Projection is a natural part of our effect on life perceptions and choices as we navigate experiential awareness. This means individually as well as collectively, with others. It is up to us to question and define the purpose of these projections in order to cultivate and refine the skills of witnessing. Acknowledging patterns of belief that influence one's reactivity or responsiveness in each situation enables a choice to modify, release, or empower the ways we affect life.

A science mind seeks to remove as much bias as possible. Yet, this can never be truly achieved due to our subjective participation that cannot be fully excluded from the context of an experience. Defining and practicing objectivity amplifies the degree of distance one perceives as a witness. For those who seek objectivity, yet tend to be more subjective, the perception may be one of less connection to the experience. This is due to the narrow self-focus that occurs in a first-person perspective that weights their senses on emotion and affectation by something acting on or to them. For those who are naturally more objective, the experience becomes an expanded vision that may reveal an even more complex layering of connections related to internal and external factors. This perspective provides an opportunity to sense a larger framework of understanding the context of self with the context of the collective or the context of the collective without the self in some scenarios.

The perceptions of every individual are marked by one's chosen roles in an experience. Roles are chosen regardless of whether they are assigned or happenstance. Each moment a role is taken on is an integrated analysis of how one is perceived, then pressured, or compelled to make a commitment to that role. This is more understandable when one practices the skill of witnessing. Every moment is a trade-off of rewards and consequences. One chooses their role based on the perceptions of these possible outcomes and acts as their own form of "weighted justice" to make the choice. The Judge and the Victim persona originate in the distortions and fixations of subjectively and objectively extreme mindsets combined with oppressive beliefs. These perceptual personas exist in each of us and it is one's choice to move beyond them through the practice of witnessing.

The greater discernment of one's own patterns, including self-talk and reactions to the world around them, cultivates a sense of synchrony in the outcomes of choices and one's life narrative. The witnessing of the narratives and experiences of others and the patterns of nature bestows the conceptual possibilities of aligning with different patterns of synchrony to achieve desired outcomes. Learning vicariously in this way offers a balance to the foundational enactment of living by trial and error. Developing discernment beyond the method of trial and error simultaneously disengages the mentality of the Judge and the Victim. This enhances a feeling of connection and alignment with one's capacity to achieve temperance and confidence to affect their own personal narrative.

To be in synchrony and to witness synchronicity in the context of one's experience, defines the skill to align gracefully in strategic choices and acceptance of outcomes. This skill is directly connected to the sense of empowerment and capability one has to be directive and receptive in their subjective and objective responses. This applies to self-witnessing and being the witness of others. Probabilities are persistent possibilities that develop theories and support those theories as accepted laws of belief. The consideration of synchrony versus coincidence is one of practiced witnessing and applied consistency in the perceptions for one or the other. Coincidence presents the question of possibility. Synchronicity presents the awareness of probability. Probability naturally increases with one's attention to intention, in order to understand the connectivity of experiences regarding the patterns witnessed and created. To change patterns and probabilities dictated by our mental and emotional constructs one must embrace the journey of the Witness. This role is a dedication expanding one's perceptions into the most profound origins of personal and collective, subjective and objective experience.

Temperance may be the most valuable guide when sensing the degrees of one's connection to the patterns in life and personal narratives. The psyche is an orb of concentric layers and every layer offers a different lens for the discernment of one's connection and active role in the experience. While knowing the farthest reaches of these concentric layers is important to understand the degree of one's "perceptive boundaries," maintaining a healthy bridge between the subjective and objective is essential to achieving integrative harmony within heart and mind. This enables success in aligning with the teachings of synchrony.

-Be bold in the endeavor to understand the origins of perception that create your personal narrative. Embrace the journey of knowing your own perceptive boundaries and continue expanding from there. Harness the potency of being the Witness and shift the patterns that do not serve the nature of your conscious being.-

XV

⚮

Empowered Humility and Adaptability

Understanding the relationship between empowered humility and adaptability is an essential concept in the path to successful endeavors in life. Life is a continual flow of change. Pressure to adapt is inherent in the biology of a species and its relationship to the earth. Each creature on the earth has a unique opportunity to cultivate skills through effort to achieve the balance of adaptability in every moment. Adaptability is not about survival alone. It can be seen in the hierarchy of consciousness as a skill that evolves our creative ability to feel, think, and manipulate our concept of self in order to attain greater contentment and security in times of change. To be effective at the kind of adaptability that brings creative opportunities for fulfillment one must harness the state of empowered humility.

Empowered humility is a balanced approach to one's role in any given moment of perceived success or setback. It requires the observation and trust in one's own power to affect circumstance and the observation of circumstance affecting oneself. It combines the recognition that we do not have dominion or power over anything but ourselves and we must decide how to use that power. Healthy humility reminds us that it is acceptable to be affected by something outside ourselves, whether that is the earth, society, or close connections with other individuals. Self-empowerment is the balance that keeps us safe from losing or giving away our power in the demands of circumstance that require humility. Excess humility decreases our sense of potency in the capacity to affect the world and others. This understanding cannot be avoided or taken to extreme assertion.

The human mind constructs and deconstructs perceptions of self, others, and the world continually. This foundational template can be hewn and refined gracefully when the concept of empowered humility is practiced and embodied.

An individual's adaptability to each arising circumstance, whether from new or old patterns of living and being, will sustainably expand with the application of empowered humility. Creative versatility then has opportunity to evolve and shift the outcomes of circumstances we exist in individually and collectively. The experience of events happening "to us" will no longer trap us in a place of submission or rebellion only, but resonate deeply into the well of our will to grow and persevere with the integrated awareness of our own power to create change in ourselves, thus effecting circumstance by our orientation to it.

The state of empowered humility is a key component of all forms of change within self and how we seek to use our power to succeed in our endeavors. Empowered humility enables diplomacy and co-creative solutions to share the conscious power we cannot deny within ourselves. Acknowledging one's own internal strengths and weaknesses, those of others on our path, as well as in the circumstances we find ourselves, sets the stage to share power or attempts to take power. To be clear, when empowered and in full knowing of self-potency, power can only be taken if it is given over willingly, but even this is an illusion. All power of self returns naturally when one acknowledges the ability to have power over oneself. The sense of empowerment does not arrive because of our witnessed affect on others or circumstances. It arrives when we witness our own ability to adapt to circumstances in a way that fortifies our relationship to our strengths and weaknesses through empowered humility and creative solutions. Many times, the reward is in the labor not the outcome.

The journey through life is an interactive experience of the self with the environment. To acknowledge oneself on this path of growing adaptation and evolving potential for creativity in consciousness is an act of self-love and self-compassion. Understanding that we all have power to share in this process of constructing and deconstructing perceptions of self, others, and the world expands our capacity to effect change and creative opportunities for sustainable fulfillment. This requires empowered humility.

~Define the power within you and listen deeply for the opportunities to adapt oneself in these times of change with compassion and diplomacy. Resolve the illusion of disparity and refine your capacity for innovative solutions that align with individual and collective fulfillment. ~

XVI

❧

Finding Your Center Within the Duality of Mind and Life

Life is full of patterns. In its most simplistic design, the pattern of duality is revealed. The divergence from one thought or one experience makes possible the perception of many other layers in our thoughts and experiences. The actions that lead from the design of those perceptions create new context in their outcomes that motivate further construction and foundation for the patterns we ultimately live by. The complexity of perceptions inspired beyond this duality can lead one down many rabbit holes of rationale. Finding and returning to one's center of truth is essential to maintaining a sense of balance when feeling the tug of war that duality and its complex of perceptual constructions may influence in the mind. This is most poignant during times of change and events that challenge one's foundations of belief.

The deepest layers of biology drive thoughts and actions for basic survival to attain protection and nourishment. After these two are established and sustainable, the design of rationale shifts to more subjective considerations around whether a thought, action, or opportunity for experience is beneficial or detrimental to the narrative one has come to believe through the process of achieving survival success. The narrative begins to take on new forms through active pursuit of subjective ideals. These beliefs and ideals may be heavily guarded by the structures of duality. Most human beings would agree that there is an inherent right and wrong when it comes to morality specifically. Where did this perception come from? What context is one basing right and wrong out of? Has the concern for right and wrong become our base assessment of any subjective experience one has?

If duality is a base design of thought and experience, like light and shadow, or sound and silence, how did the perception of accuracy in one's alignment to right and wrong come about? Perhaps the narrative of religion defines this or the laws, declared by culture and society, are the origin of acceptance. Perhaps, it is inherent in the construct of the brain's evolution and grasped through the process of mindful awareness. It seems that right versus wrong is far more conditional and easily manipulated by the perceptions of the mind in contrast to the pure neutral duality of the experiential light, shadow, sound, and silence. To be conditional in one's mental rationale is paralleled by the dual opportunity to be unconditional; to judge or not judge, to have attachment to an idea or belief versus detachment from an idea or belief. The point is that the true patterns of duality in existence are inherently neutral unless the perception is applied to them as right or wrong; acceptable or unacceptable. They are as inevitable as life and death, regardless of how one feels about it.

Unveiling the practical function of duality is essential because it creates an opportunity to redefine our terms and understanding of those terms to a more neutral beginning in the design of our personal construct of beliefs, beyond the initial moments of divergence when assessing an idea, action, or possibility. Consider the use of beneficial or detrimental, harmonic or dissonant, and aligned or not aligned. These terms open up the dimensional awareness of conditionality with consideration for how ideas or beliefs serve one's perceived path to achieving greater ease in the process of survival and beyond this to many subjective layers of thinking and feeling. Through this refining of terms and acceptance of duality, the cycle of return to one's center of truth may be imprinted with greater ease and less conflict of rationale.

As a species advancing in conscious awareness there are many opportunities and challenges to the framework one lives from. The tug of war within spurs us to choose each fork in the road of the paths we walk. The imprints of outside voices and events can be overwhelming and obscuring of our own true nature, especially when many are living from the assumed conditionality of right versus wrong. The most graceful way to quiet the noise outside or within is to release attachment to the experiences during one's inner conflict long enough to ask the questions of one's knowing heart and bodily instinct. Does this align with me? How does this thought or belief serve me at this time? How does it serve me in the future? Is this thought or ideal mine or someone else's?

Bodily awareness is key. The resonance of feeling sensation in the chest, belly, and head are most common when seeking the uplift of "yes" or the dense pressure of "no." There are times when these sensations occur simultaneously in the same or different parts of the body. When this happens it's ok to acknowledge the answer is inconclusive and inquire again, at another time. Sometimes our integration and understanding is still digesting and the simplistic yes or no are not currently conducive to that process. More investigation of one's beliefs, ideals, resistance, or ignorance to information may be required for clarity in the assessment. This is the beautiful journey of expanding conscious awareness.

Finding one's center of truth is the essential embodiment of one's integrity for how they create and direct themselves in the world. Knowing and maintaining connection to the core of self enables more profound understanding in the truths of others while securing accountability for self and the empowerment to co-create more effective communication. This in turn supports the refinement of design in personal and shared structures of ideals and beliefs.

~Come into the core of your inner knowing and embrace the cord of truth. Release the pressures of rationale and unify beyond the divisiveness of duality, to listen. Seek balance in service to self and innovation in the service to others. ~

XVII

❧

Validation in Personal Values and Becoming the Authentic Self

Value systems are the foundation of how we seek and discern validation with the world and ourselves. Throughout the maturation process of life, validation outside oneself may have a stronger influence on the alignment, enactment, and adherence to different values. Introspection to understand the purpose, benefit, detriment, and progress of these values is essential to discovering the authentic self and clarifying the resonant truth in one's values as self-validation. It is important to go beyond validation from others influencing the identification one feels in a value and value system. Letting go of fear and indifference to expand outside the comfort zone of what we think we know of ourselves is paramount in revealing the value system that establishes success for becoming one's most authentic self.

In childhood we are like a sponge soaking up information in the world, our family, and our closest relationships. As one grows the conceptual balancing of distinguishing who we are in the context of these relationships and the world is constantly changing, even without our awareness of it. Different friends, events, and societal trends heavily influence thoughts, feelings, and decisions we make. Imprinting continues as a part of experiential memory, cause and effect principles, and how we learn as beings for an individual's entire life. What we choose to analyze, integrate, and transmute in any experience will effect how we operate in similar circumstances, roles we repeat in life for self or others, and how one shares their story revealing the values associated with it.

With any imprint it is essential to ask if it resonates or "feels like ours." Does it remind us of someone else we learned that value from or experienced that imprint with? Are we acting out of this memory or imprint without really choosing to see how this action benefits or conflicts with who we are? How does one feel about the perception of value in the experience, how it pertains to others, and how it pertains to self? Initiating questions about one's values and value system is key to understanding oneself in order to share that authenticity with others, for achieving success in what we align with most and seek to create, and to refine one's capacity to respond more than react to repeated circumstances throughout life.

The value systems of an individual, generations of individuals, and larger populations in civilizations advocating free thought and innovation vary significantly. When considering one's values and the experience of validation in the collective field it is most beneficial to acknowledge that differences are not always as polarized as it may initially feel. Many experiences have underlying similarities, yet all the other factors of conscious awareness or subconscious imprinting change the outcome of how values are embodied and upheld. One cannot truly judge the introspective machinations of another if they have not walked in their shoes. The act of judging others for their values without attending to introspection on one's own value system and the equal willingness to seek understanding in why another upholds their values only blocks the creative opportunity to assess one's own values more deeply, as well as the possibility that both individuals' value systems may actually be more similar in their intent and function than assumed.

By choosing to only listen to what one wants to hear or by placing oneself in a small field of influence for the sake of validation, the opportunity for self-awareness, growth, and refinement of values will be limited. Likewise, when repeating the same acts over, and over again, based in autopilot without clarity of purpose and values, one cannot expect a different experience will occur. Pushing away opportunities to expand beyond detrimental and impertinent imprints for an individual's personal experience of life reduces the capacity for clarifying the authentic self and achieving self-validation, unattached to the validation given by others.

The strongest form of validation comes from self-validation alone, with clarity from introspection for that validation. Validation from others for confirmation of shared values is secondary yet magnifies the effect of carrying those values together. Mutual validation is the doorway to co-creative opportunities, bestowing a sense of support and ease in unity. Differing values also open the doorway to co-creative opportunities maintaining a dynamic give and take of acknowledgment for other possibilities and the call to innovate multidimensional value systems that achieve mutually successful outcomes. The art of compromise is only mastered by those who understand this.

Different generations carry their seeds of wisdom within their values. The enactment of those values may vary in strategy based on the validation by others in the population for better or worse. The face of change always affects the values of those involved. A new perspective proliferating for dominance may be naïve or highly informed. Without communication with self and with others, understanding may not be achieved. A lack of honoring the wisdom others carry in their differences sets a stage for conflict and disappointment on all sides.

The goal of values is to establish a working agreement with self for how to act and be in the world. Sharing these values with others to reach an understanding of how to operate together for successful outcomes that bring fulfillment is the path to expanding the capacity of a collective to operate in the world. If there are no values, there is little introspection or concern for innovation and like the withering of a plant in drought will come the loss of civilization.

~Center yourself in the resonance of your perceived value system. Deepen and refine the potency of your authentic self and expand the brilliance of delightful wisdom in our collective.~

XVIII

❧

Harnessing the Senses

Being in body bestows upon us the world of the senses. The innate 5 senses to the human body and the 6th sense of intuition create a profound system of language to analyze, act upon, affect the intensity of, and collect experiences with, as memory. Sensory awareness can be pleasurable, painful, confounding, and indistinguishable depending on the experience and an individual's attunement to the language of bodily senses. Evolutionary biology associates the initial sense of pain recognition as the rudimentary sense related to survival. If focused upon, this sense becomes belief, which governs impulse and imprinting to dominate one's perceptions in their body and in the world. Since then, epigenetic science has revealed that the mind and body also have the power to focus on pleasure and neutrality as a way to orient base drives and perceptions that govern the experience of sensory memory and the journey of life. Learning to harness the 6 senses for healing is a profound path that enables transformative regeneration by resetting inherent reflexes, impulses, and draining thoughts or emotions that lead to loss of mental, emotional, physical, and spiritual health.

In every moment, in body, awareness is happening. When the mind isn't paying attention, the body is still receiving, processing, and storing sensory awareness. The body also listens to the mind and compensates in form and breath to thoughts and emotional cognizance. The power of enjoyable or stressful thoughts cause changes in breathing, blood pressure, and oxygenation. The way one feels open to connect with others in a safe healthy way or the contraction and internalization of defensiveness changes the posture of the spine and the tone of muscles in the limbs ready to relax or protect the core. Behavioral cues change from momentary to habitual when underlying imprints of experiences dictate an individual's orientation to self, connection with others, and their environment regardless of admission to self or others about those inherent thoughts and feelings. These subconscious cues may greatly shift the outcome of one's desires and endeavors as fulfilled or unfulfilled.

Once introspection and active effort are put forth to accept, heal, and re-embody one's orientation to self and the world, profound shifts in an individual's narrative of life can occur. In the same way, major injuries, crises, loss, and periods of survival mode can change one's experiential beingness and sense of life. Bodywork therapies, holistic counseling, spiritual practices, and healthy lifestyle routines also have great power to change and restore functionality and freedom in one's experience of life in body. The key is the sensory self. Awakening the acuity of each sense and modulating the potential capacity to be affected by each sense must be a committed journey if one seeks the mastery of embodiment.

The path of the senses may be very intense for some at varying phases of cultivation, healing, and integrating tools for magnifying or subduing the senses at will. By opening to the teaching of one's senses, the animal self is brought into conversation and partnership with the cerebral dominance most scientists distinguish as primary to being human. The concept exists that a spiritual form roots itself in a body with primal instincts creating the possibility of the animal and human self and is worth considering. If function equals form in a path of evolution, the greater capacity for function in receiving and utilizing sensory awareness confirms the current hierarchy of dominant species and the path forward to augmenting form through expanding the function of the senses. The more we numb, ignore, and deplete our senses the less functional we are in mind, heart, and body. Senses, thoughts, and emotions are meant to be tools that inform one's strategies for living. When these tools are unrefined and imbalanced in their power to affect the way one forms imprints and makes choices, voluntarily and involuntarily, the outcomes in experience will occur with the redundance of disappointment or short-term fulfillment.

The clarity and potency of true free will cannot be achieved when an individual lives only from the mind or only from emotions. To live only from spirit is to discount the sensory gift of being in body. Living only from the 5 physical senses disregards the integration of understanding and actively choosing beyond impulse how to respond to the world. The essence of life is captivating because of one's ability to listen to their senses. Intuition is the 6th sense of embodiment. With intuition, one trusts a center of knowing. This center of knowing is found at the bridge between the spirit and the senses of the physical body. Conscious analytical thought is not required to hear this sense of wisdom. Analytical thought is how we structure the input and sensory imprints we receive. The mind is a weigh station that estimates the load of information and regulates the intensity and frequency of preponderance on that input. Intention in the mind directs further attention in the mind, heart, and body.

Redefining one's relationship to embodiment through regular attention to the senses from a state of mental curiosity and emotional exploration engages the embrace of vitality and enables deeper acknowledgment of how this information serves us in what we seek to create in the experience of humanness. Choosing neutrality and observation after pain arises, to move beyond suffering to the focus of healing and allowing relief and pleasure to be restored, is a powerful tool cultivated by harnessing the senses. This practice enables the discovery and refinement of our most authentic self.

~Let your senses engage a deeper understanding of wisdom within you. Refine the trust in yourself and the gifts of embodiment to experience life in a state of curiosity and receptivity that empowers rejuvenation. Activate the intention to embrace an evolution of form in function and restore the wealth of the body, mind, heart, and spirit. ~

XIX

⁜

Integrity and Leading with Intention

The path to achieving what we want in life is marked with obstacles that create resistance and problem-solving opportunities. The forks in the road of a journey can challenge one's sense of self. These crossroads may bring us to question the depth of desire one carries to continue the pursuit of living achievements. Diversions from one path to another in that may reveal a choice to sacrifice one's integrity for the sake of winning or in the face of losing. Your alignment with your core truths and the enactment of those beliefs by leading with intention is essential to maintaining integrity with self and with others, regardless of perceived winning or losing. Leading with intention to honor one's integrity and the integrity of others enables self-respect, mutual respect, and healthy foundations for empowering experiential outcomes.

Integrity is intimately intertwined within self-worth and how one feels when experiencing achievement or the struggle to achieve desired outcomes. If an individual feels they have compromised part of their integrity to meet a goal the satisfaction of meeting that goal is lessened. If an individual is struggling to achieve a desired outcome, questioning one's parameters of integrity and reconsidering the value of integrity may arise. Holding the line of clear intention may falter, further clouding direction for how to progress. When intentions are unclear an individual is prone to submitting to a path that does not honor one's integrity, to the will of others, or to shutting down altogether. The alignment of principles may shift in the creative process toward finding solutions to meet a goal, yet integrity does not have to be compromised if what is learned in the re-orientation of principles harmonizes with and individual's core truths and empowers conscientious self-worth.

Leading with integrity and intention is essential to feeling empowered in one's choices and upholding self-worth in any circumstance. No matter the outcome of an endeavor, being in alignment with and acting from one's core truths maintains self-trust. Holding clear intentions and returning to these acknowledged intentions, even in the struggle to achieve, is the foundation of how we value our efforts and actions when striving for successful outcomes. If devaluation of intention and efforts prevail, a perceived self-betrayal is inevitable. This self-betrayal may be miniscule or enormous in the narrative of life, but the culmination of many small betrayals will undermine self-trust and self-worth, perhaps even more than one significant betrayal of the self. It all depends on the individual and their alignment to the principles that define their character. It depends on the foundation of one's intentions and integrity throughout a life. Either way, self-trust and self-worth are required in the symbiotic relationship of living with integrity and leading with intention. When the mind is lost in the mire of rationale, the way to center your focus is to return to the core truth of your intention and follow the path of greatest integrity from there. Satisfaction with self is an essential component to the acceptance of any outcome and acceptance supports intentions and actions for better outcomes.

Leading with intention aligned with our integrity defines the potency of any act that comes from those intentions. Self-empowerment by living one's truth intentionally and sharing those intentions put in place to honor those truths with others structures the design of an individual's life, efforts, and endeavors. Acknowledging self-trust and self-worth naturally advocates the actions required to achieve fulfilling outcomes, to redirect strategies or goals as needed, and to accurately assess whether one's principles and actions are serving the tenets of empowered living. Living in empowered self-trust and intention every day attunes individual potential to manifest desired outcomes in the narrative of life. Resilience and the will to heal from disappointment, loss, and the many painful challenges of life are easier found in the individuals who lead with integrity. Honoring self and others as well as the challenges of life intentionally expands the possibilities for creative solutions, clarity of responsibility in distorted circumstances, and mutual opportunities to build understanding and respect in communication.

When everything beyond self is silent and removed, how one feels about themselves dictates how one trusts their own integrity and diligence of will to choose between the paths that arise in the external world. If jaded, regaining self-trust and self-worth requires the acknowledgment of an individual's core truths and the alignment with those truths in efforts, actions, and communications. It is best to begin by leading with intention in the smallest tasks and then the greater endeavors. Leading with intention and honoring your integrity is a practice in every moment. Embracing a sustainable path of self-worth and resilience for the challenges of life requires trust and acknowledgment of the truest identity that defines your center of being.

~Know thyself, love thyself, and be thyself in the rise of success and the fall of adversity. Seek to learn more than you know of yourself in every journey and outcome in the narrative of your life. Harness the potency of intentional living and perpetuate the sacredness of personal integrity. ~

XX

⁐

The Power of
Acknowledgment

In a society built on striving and a world that invites opportunity for understanding, acknowledgment is an essential component of healthy confirmation, connection, and motivation. Directing one's awareness to how and when acknowledgment of self and others is due by relevance or compelled as an offering, creates the opportunity for greater clarity, growth, and mutual fulfillment. How often in a day or a week do you openly acknowledge yourself in positive ways for who you are and what you feel purpose in? How often do you acknowledge the darker, confusing, and hard parts about who you are or how your behaviors affect life around you? How often do you acknowledge these positive and negative perceptions about others in your life or in your world?

Acknowledgment is like a mirror, a place of awareness where one cannot ignore what they witness and the beliefs that grow from that image. Honest neutral statements that express what one sees in self or another, will plant seeds for empowerment and opportunities to feel confirmation. Even if the acknowledgment is about a struggle or dissonance witnessed within self or other(s), a sense of being seen and heard naturally arises. This is very different than harsh declarations that are presumptive or intend to demean oneself or other(s). The language of true acknowledgment is always accompanied by the intention to support an individual's process toward fulfillment or celebrate an individual's accomplishments. In a goal oriented society seeking the bottom line, acts of acknowledgment throughout the journey to that goal are often missed and persistent deferral of opportunities to acknowledge when the framed bottom line isn't achieved yet, is unfortunately commonplace. When we acknowledge ourselves or others the momentum of motivation for self-awareness, self-trust, self-introspection, and clarity for action thrives. This applies to cultivating understanding within self, relationships with others, and confirmation of roles or purpose in one's endeavors to benefit connection and one's sense of fulfillment.

Acknowledgment can be the key that opens the door when someone feels shutdown, misunderstood, or neglected. It is an offering and it is a tool for clarifying reactionary moments in conflict. It can be a powerful invitation to step into a place of honoring oneself and others. This is magnified when all individuals in any circumstance are open enough to acknowledge others for the positive attributes and intentions they are attempting to communicate or exemplify. The empowerment to collaborate, find a better way to accomplish mutual understanding, and shift the resistance around being insulted or infringed upon, increases the probability of harmonic outcomes for an individual or group.

Developing the language of acknowledgment is an essential part of ensuring receptivity on delivery. Sentences that own the experience of what one is witnessing are most productive, such as "I hear this.." "I see this about....[you, myself]" "From what I have witnessed..". Including a follow up "check in" question if it feels pertinent in circumstances regarding compliments or understandings, such as "Do you feel or see this?" "Do you agree?" creates mobility and mutuality in the exchange. This approach to communication can shift ones entire view of self, others, and world-views at any given time in this journey of life. Acknowledgement is part of healthy reinforcement for the foundations of self, endeavors in relationship with others, and roles of purpose that arise and shift in any dream we seek to create. The toil of blood, sweat, and tears, the constant laboring to provide and procure for self, and/or others, and the insidious toll on mental, emotional, and physical wellbeing that comes with surviving, striving, and recognizing fulfillment in our creative process can feel like a hamster wheel or a marathon, draining a sense of purpose, without moments of acknowledgment from oneself and from others witnessing or taking part in the fruit of our labors.

Even if that mental, emotional, physical, or spiritual fruit isn't ripe, every integral part is worth acknowledging. From preparing the ground to sowing the seed, to each stage of tending that ensures replenishment at its peak. There will always be loss, failed plantings, and unforeseen conditions that change the needs of any growth process. It is especially then, that acknowledgments can be the weighted feather that balances or tips the scales, in favor of passion to endure and surrender to the transformative cycles of beingness.

~Defer the preconceiving judge and take the time to witness. Let your heart and mind be open to receive and clarify your intentions. Let respect and acknowledgment for the experience of humanness guide communication and behold the way- to integrity- to honor all in creation.~

XXI

❦

The Constellation Effect in Self and Relationships

As we dream into the night sky, the stars illuminate patterns on the canvas of existence. Our mind's eye connects the dots and whole narratives unfold for the influence of perception, allegories to our experience, no matter how young or old. The common denominator is always the one listening, being affected, seeking wisdom in the overlay of one story to another, and these stories to oneself. This is a constellation. It is one field of connection among infinite fields of connection on the backdrop of a unified verse.

Relationships are constellations. They are fields of connection across space with narratives that unfold between the self and the non-self, self with self, self with others, others with others, and non-others with others. The "non-" is inanimate, conceptual thought, unattached from emotion, inorganic forms, and inventions in existence that one feels a relationship to. Relationship can include nonattachment, denial, and disregard to any animate being, inorganic form, or concept under the title of "non-". The origin of all things is the same and relationships are inherent because of this. This means that the more one accesses the deepest source and wisdom of the authentic self, the more clarity and refinement of intention will potentiate and magnetize the relationships that support, protect, nourish, and heal the experience and manifestation of one's personal narrative. This is the art of witnessing, learning from, and redesigning your own constellations throughout life, illuminating the sky of your mind.

In the everyday life, constellations effect how we feel about ourselves, how one gravitates towards certain patterns in relationship with others, beliefs that control the perceptions in one's reality, and events that bring outcomes based on intention and awareness of self and/or others. The correlation between lifestyle, work, and stress, between dreams to achieve for self, family, the world, are a woven fabric that reveals patterns of self. These can each be broken down into simple 1:1 relationship for analysis of how they function and whether they are serving the deepest sense of self. These relationships can be illuminated and redesigned by shifting one's orientation to them, opening a path for the image and the story perceived, to change. Stories like these are everyday but may be commonly undervalued besides the glorified tales of heroism. It is naturally within consciousness to sort, process, integrate, and refine approaches to life with greater efficiency, no matter how mundane or daunting the task. All sentient beings exhibit this ingenuity. The art applies when attention to this process is cultivated and the will to precision is pursued.

In every constellation an effect is exponential. Shifting the orientation to one point of reference ripples out across every other connection causing some degree of awareness and association. The catalyst is the acute comprehension of a choice, the feeling out of how a relationship to a belief, other, non-other, or self, is in service to one's dream. The dream birthed from the origins of the psyche for the narrative of one's life and their role in existence. Relationships are cords of connection that resonate with how often and what one gives to them. This is how they survive, thrive, or fade and die. For better or worse is a subjective question only an individual can answer directly. It may be echoed by others with subjective feelings about the connection indirectly. At times, this echo may not come, nor is it required of the non-self, other, or non-other at the opposite end of the cord in question. Changing a relationship or refining alignment within a constellation may require the simplest task of saying "yes" or "no", or a phrase that declares the truth in the heart of how one feels and how one wants to feel, how one wants to heal, or how one seeks to overcome, to release, or to attain. The power of truth in one's voice combined with the will to feel and redefine orientation to what is illuminated in one's body-mind, seeds the activation of intention.

The relationship of an individual to their own intentions is not an exception to clarifying and manifesting the dream of the psyche and one's role in existence. This may be the most essential treasure that reveals the origins of the authentic self and its connection to the source of the universe. The perception of time itself creates a field of constellations to access within the mind and heart that defines and structures a narrative, yet its role is always subject to an individual's orientation to it. The graceful embrace or the fear of time and the attachment or detachment to grace, fear, or time, are all cords in a field of constellation interdependent and interacting with one another. It is abstract and yet distinguishable by the language of feeling and the language of seeing. Learning to communicate these tangible sensations is the framework of sentient embodiment.

The network of friends, family, social contacts, and romantic relationships are more complex constellations, subjectively speaking. The influence of these cords in one's life have some of the most lasting effects. They influence and manipulate the vision of oneself in many ways that may support or hinder an individuals connection to the deepest origins of their authentic self. Yet, the allowance of this by lack of awareness or active awareness is dependent on attention to self and a willingness to query for intentional refinement. Seeking honor, transparency, and ingenuity consolidates the will to harness one's own creative empowerment in order to direct their personal narrative. The work of constellation is a multidimensional process. It is a conceptualization of life happening every moment with the viewer as the ultimate point of relativity. Understanding this reveals the mirror of thought and emotion, of events and outcomes that flow in a feedback system resonant in the cords of an individual's relationship to all other perspectives in the web of consciousness. It is karma and dharma. It is cause and effect and it is polarity of opposites along with the origins of unity.

~Reach out into the sky of mind and deep to the peace in your heart. Feel the frequency of every moment in relationship with your authentic self. Let this resonance guide ingenuity to see higher planes of relativity and witness a symphony of stars unveil each path to harmony.~

XXII

֍

Soul Contracts and Closure Beyond Grief and Loss

Throughout life we reveal the elements and identity of who we are and who we share life with. The relationship to ourselves and to others weaves into the fabric of our perceptions and challenges us to acknowledge that our beliefs about others and ourselves dictate the freedom, fulfillment, and security we hold the ability to attain. The binding of beliefs and the lack of awareness in how we create and/or serve attachments to others directly relates to our intensity of and perpetuation of grief or a sense of loss. Reaching a state of closure can be daunting when the maze of one's mind and the perceived contractual obligations to self or others stands in the way.

Soul contracts may be subconscious or conscious agreements with oneself or another made as a negotiated trade off. Every day we think about and act on the agreements made to be a part of one's chosen lifestyle, to surrender to or endure external factors beyond one's control, and to recognize how our roles and actions affect others. Every day we choose to ignore or to face discomfort we feel or to embrace and acknowledge the strength and contentment we have in our experience. Every day we choose to accept or resist the depth of connection one has the capacity to build with family, friends, work, and society.

The agreements with self are the first contracts we make in the world as we unveil the feeling of what we have and have not agreed to in our journey of self-awareness. The agreements with others are secondary contracts that can only be fulfilled to the extent that one can remain true to the contracts with self and the capacity we have to any contract with self and others. This means beyond the idealism of what one wants to be capable of. Unconscious agreements can feel most insidious when it comes to perceived bondage in an agreement to achieve the goal of whatever that contractual agreement dictates. Contractual agreements are defined by thoughts, feelings, and ideals blended with personal principles, abilities, and realistic projections of one's capacity to achieve the desired outcome. Knowing what that desired outcome is, is imperative to completing or absolving the contract and integrating or nullifying its' purpose.

Some contracts are placed on us by others that we have not consciously agreed to. These are the most essential contracts to acknowledge, dissolve, and release. The perception that anyone has power over you or that their demands of you are required to be fulfilled is an illusion. The primary contracts with self will safeguard and clarify what one commands of themselves to assert their own will to break, deny, or dissolve the contracts others place upon them. This includes the conscious secondary agreements one makes with others that oppose one's primary agreements with self.

The perception of bondage to an agreement is based on emotional attachment that is exacerbated by confusion and cyclical tapes in the mind. Grief and loss of connection, in life or death, is a prominent place where arguments with self and the re-negotiation of contracts with self or with others are played out. The circumstance of a dissolving relationship or experience in the death of a loved one can be overwhelming and confusing emotionally, driving an individual to hold on to certain contractual agreements that can no longer be fulfilled for the sake of an individual's desire to remain attached to the one lost. Moving beyond grief and loss requires an individual to embrace gratitude for what was shared. This also means acknowledging the change of circumstances around loss as an opportunity to continue in life, with the memories and teachings bestowed, and to find closure in unfulfilled contracts. Finding clarity in the agreements with self, integrating the accomplishments from secondary contracts with the one lost, and releasing residual contracts that were unfulfilled and can no longer be completed without the presence of both individuals, are all a part of seeking closure in order to feel at ease with the new circumstances one finds themselves in.

Experiencing grief and loss for another is an inseparable context for the acknowledgment of self and the opportunity to redefine one's contracts with self and life. Grief and loss show us ourselves because the deepest wells of suffering exist in the attachments of the mind we are faced with and often consumed by. Someone can be in emotional bondage to their self as much as they can be by agreement to another. The way to closure is through autonomy of self. Chosen agreements with self are the primary foundation of how one operates and applies these agreements to move effectively through a life of changing circumstance. Re-negotiating agreements is always an option, for better or worse. One must choose wisely with intentional awareness of their own will and capacity to meet their primary agreements with self and secondary agreements with others. Any soul contract may be accepted or absolved once the clarity of an individual's realistic desire and ability to achieve the purpose of that contract is acknowledged.

When someone has died and is no longer present to demand contract fulfillment or maintain progress toward a desired dream made together, it is time to release oneself of the contract and strengthen contracts with self to live forward. Closure is a step by step, day by day, process of relinquishing attachment. To relinquish attachment and the bondage of contracts to another is not devaluing or denial of love and appreciation. The release of attachment is an act of self-empowerment that transforms the experience of loss, confusion, guilt, shame, and grief by offering an objective view that is realistic to the distance felt between oneself and another.

~Self- love, nourishment, and release of emotional bondage are all essential for self-empowerment, clarity, and peace in the wake of loss. They are acts of acknowledgement for the love, attentiveness, and receptivity to share in the relationship one has put in, now returned to self. This is the cycle of love, of exchange, of creativity, and transformation. ~

XXIII

❦

Vulnerability and Resilience with an Open Heart

The power of an open heart catalyzes the opportunity for sharing and receiving abundant fulfillment. On the journey to open one's heart for fulfillment the choice to explore and to create in the world as an individual and in relationship with others increases one's perceptions of vulnerability. Perceptions of joy, ambition, contentment, security, loss, lack of success, disappointment for expectations unmet, and nuances in a perceived lack of control are all part of the experience in this process. Life events that feel traumatic or unsatisfying can influence an individual to shut down and isolate as an effort to defend and protect the perceived parts of self that are being challenged in the face of vulnerability.

At its' core the challenge is an opportunity to deepen into one's understanding of the resistance in order to create more effectively. It may be motivating us to place proper boundary for self and others, or to augment balance where it is lacking, and to question one's perceptions about the fears, disappointment, anger, and righteousness that may be demanding a total shut down, escape, or backlash reaction to the experience of being vulnerable. By deepening one's relationship to the authentic self and empowering trust within, the power to move beyond resistance and to transmute perceived threats is embodied. Then, the trade-off of choosing the path of an open heart and vulnerability may be viewed as the cultivation of resilience.

Resilience is how we survive not only physically but emotionally, mentally, and spiritually. Throughout a life, cultivation of dependence on resilience may become partial and lacking wholeness. Reliance on protecting only the primary parts of self that one perceives as necessity, can divide the intentional focus of cultivating wholeness which enables reliance on all aspects of oneself. This is evident when one component of how an individual creates in life is successful in resilience while others are diminished. Someone can be great at surviving physically, yet low in the reserves of spiritual perseverance. Another can be well developed in mental fortitude when connecting with others and strategizing successful endeavors, yet poor in emotional stamina and empathy when developing personal relationships and embracing the wisdom of the bodily senses.

As the human species advances technologically, the reliance on mental faculties will continue to dominate. Living life from a cerebral, reductionist, and rationalizing foundation severs the sentient cords of feeling, instinct, and intuition that reveal an expansive network of creative skills to meet life's basic demands and denies achievements of growth through function in a holistic way. It is the nature of the mind to seek control, understanding, and affect when exploring the world and chaperoning connection with self and others. It is the nature of the heart to feel affected and to contain the sensory experience of inspiration through a relationship with self and others.

When the perception of vulnerability arises, the compensatory mechanism of defense is a basic imprint of the survival mind. It is the nature of the survival mind to seek control at all costs in the attempt to persist "as is" in the experience of life. Superseding this urge enables a deepening into the experience of the feelings and thoughts associated with the catalyst of vulnerability. This requires the acceptance of change as a versatile teacher and a willingness to refine one's awareness in the context of that change. Engaging the curiosity of the mind to reveal what the heart contains and how to utilize it with resilience is the way to aspiring beyond just surviving into the art of thriving. Thriving requires the intentional cultivation of multifaceted skills in order to maintain integrity with the authentic self. This pursuit of awareness evolves the dynamic of existence.

Choosing to live life with an open heart and trusting in resilience through the experience of vulnerability is an essential skill in this endeavor. The most profound experiences of fulfillment in the human journey reside in the knowing, receiving, and giving of love to self, others, the world, and a higher spiritual power. The teachings of love come in many forms. The beliefs of the individual are reflected in the intensity and frequency of love as it is experienced. It is the mind that chaperones, structures, and defines what has, is, and will be enabled for exchange. No matter the traumas, losses, and unmet expectations of an individual, the potency of love still exists to be received, cultivated, and shared.

The mask of vulnerability sheds its' skin as the layers of the psyche push forth for acknowledgment, illumination, and enlightenment. The most alchemical transformations are activated by the resolve to embrace one's power and to acknowledge the embodiment of love's teachings as the source of that power. This requires the will to receive, the immersion within that container of feeling, and the will to expand the capacity of perceived limitations within. It requires ones' attention to refinement of mental and emotional filters that allow free passage into and out of this rhythmic reservoir of self. The courage to face vulnerability has no root without love to draw upon. The rewards of protecting oneself can feel hollow and draining to achieve without a deeper valuation of purpose for the efforts of thriving in lieu of surviving.

Loving oneself, the essence of life, and carrying love for others invigorates and magnifies the experience of success when the call to learn from vulnerability or the perceived need for protection unfolds. Choosing to live and love with an open heart, requests one's willingness to experience vulnerability and trust in the resilience of one's power to adapt. It requests that we accept change, loss, death, and the challenges to refine meaning in what we think we know of ourselves. The emotional catharsis of the heart is the fire of transmutation that opens the threshold to the psyche's evolution.

~Lower the gates to your fortress and bridge the gap between heart and mind. Let embodiment inform you and generate the potency to thrive from your authentic core. Dig down into the root and illuminate a path to create, beyond fear, with the brilliance of love and trust.~

XXIV

❦

Honorable Transparency, Truth, and Lying

What is honorable transparency? What is truth? How do we define lying if we have not defined what truth and transparency mean? Truth is constructed by relativity to circumstance and agreements with others about what is perceived. Fact is defined as undeniable truth based in physical or recordable evidence. It is not uncommon for relative perceptions of truth to be misconstrued as fact without evidence. Honorable transparency requires one to reveal the differences between facts and perceived truths, out of respect for others witnessing that transparency maintain their own capacity to evaluate and discern the meaning, application, and effects of information shared. The act of lying may be defined as representing the opposite of the truth or facts of a situation, modifying these facts or truths, or intentionally withholding truths and facts to manipulate the perceptions and responses of others evaluating the information given.

In the efforts of evolving consciousness collectively, increasing one's awareness beyond the base drives of survival and emotional reactivity is essential. The pursuit of measurable fact and discernment of philosophical truth can offer allies for refining perceptions of self, others, and the world. Accepting there may be more than one perspective of truth enables healthier communication with self and others. The art of striving for healthy communication and outcomes that align with one's personal code is achieved through honorable transparency. "Your bond is your word" is an old saying about building trust and loyalty with others but it directly affects the perception of oneself as well. To honor oneself in the highest regard one must be in alignment with their own philosophical truth, balanced by the facts of situational awareness. Even if one does not believe in truth, loyalty and honoring can still be maintained by openly sharing this belief to achieve transparency with others, so they may evaluate and better understand one's responses to a situational construct. Lying about one's truth or beliefs to self or with others creates division and conflict internally, externally, or both, that breaks down one's sense of value and connection with the authentic self. The farther an individual is from connection and loyalty to the authentic self, the more distorted their perceptions are of life, relationships, and outcomes they affect. It is not uncommon for the most disconnected individuals to be compulsive liars, narcissists, or any other shade on the spectrum of sociopathic disorder.

Individuals who seek truth and transparency to create strong bonds of loyalty, security, and mutual agreements, sense the lies, manipulation, denial, and misguided intentions of others. This skill strengthens as their attunement to transparency and evaluating the fulfillment or disconnection between thoughts, behaviors, and intentions are refined. With the expansion of awareness, complex understandings of a multidimensional world with many co-creative factors that affect an individual's perspective on what is true in any moment, and what is not, become more apparent. How much an individual has the power to see, evaluate, and grasp, through acceptance of understanding, dictates the relative truth surmised from the facts and one's response to the facts.

If truth is relative to an individual state of awareness, is lying relative also? On the path to discovery and understanding a life circumstance, relationship, or sense of self, identity shifts form in alignment with an individual's degree of understanding, layers of information revealed, and changes in situational perspective over time. All these factors create, modify, and deconstruct one's perception of a "whole truth" through the framework of relativity. Facts remain the same but an individual's perception of them may change, as well as, their degree of value and affect, which share an interdependent relationship with perception. An individual's core sense of belief about anything may stay the same but it has the power to change. Acknowledging this change of perception with clear intention is not lying about one's truth. Lying reveals itself through the intent to manipulate facts to self, or others, or attempts to hide or deny one's representation of perceptions to self or others.

Cognitive dissonance between facts and philosophical truths, repetitive behaviors, and misaligned statements perpetuate the experience of conflict, resistance, and distrust with self and others. The authentic self is very sensitive to the awareness of discernible truth, transparency, and deceit when the smoke and mirrors of emotional reactivity and forced denial is removed. Every individual grapples with their own smoke and mirror effect that leads to personal cognitive dissonance because of their own experiential encoding and attachment to working beliefs that are beneficial or detrimental to achieving a fulfilling exchange with self, others, and endeavors in life. Working beliefs are an essential part of how an individual learns and expands their awareness, enabling a higher capacity for directing their will for creative solutions and empowering outcomes.

Honorable transparency and compassionate communication build the foundations of trust and loyalty with self and others continually throughout life. Those that are unable to harness these skills will perpetuate long term and repetitive conflict, distrust, broken loyalties, and divergence from stronger connections that have the power to nourish and support the tangible experiences of harmony and unity in one's personal narrative. Choosing integrity, curiosity, and compassionate transparency of self and others fortifies an individual's skill for discernment beyond judgment, clarity with projections, and a balance of expectations in every circumstance within self or others. Taking the time to step back and witness self, others, and the dynamic of situations is key to evaluate and apply all these factors for building trust through honorable transparency in the search for truth.

~Open your keen Eye to the relativity of perspective. Discern the veils that shroud truth in any moment, sensing magnetic alignment with the compass of the authentic self. Let honorable transparency illuminate the path to healthy, enduring relationships that transcend cognitive dissonance and empower sustainable trust and respect. ~

XXV

꙰

On Worthiness

Worthiness is an experience created by the values and reflections an individual carries about themselves and the world. Worthiness is a feeling that cannot be given to you. It can only be illuminated within by acts of acknowledgment. Acknowledgement of self-value is the primary foundation of any feeling, emotion, or thought within self that has meaning and purpose. Acknowledgment from others in the framework of our lives is secondary to the foundations of feeling esteem in one's worthiness. Receiving this influence from others can only occur if one allows their influence to have effect on the core construct of how one values self. Worthiness is a choice. It is a choice to honor that one has meaning and purpose. It is an act of will that protects and inspires every individual to trust their inherent value in life, no matter the experiences of internal conflict and external perceptions or recognition by other individuals.

The experience of worthiness can take many dimensions through-out life circumstances, perceived failures and successes in endeavors for self, interpersonal relationships that are supportive, abusive, or neglectful, and emotional overwhelm in life phases with high demand for learning, processing, and applying one's truth. The essence of self-value trumps every outcome in life whether perceived consciously or subconsciously by an individual. Acknowledging one's own self worth and understanding how it is defined and distinguished within oneself is elemental to utilizing and remembering one's own power during life experiences challenge, disregard, and/or degrade the feeling of worthiness. Worthiness is the truth of one's own will to stand in their power. By honoring the core of oneself as always worthy, no matter the failures or denials in life or by others, worthiness can act as a shield to fortify the boundaries of self from the attack of others and a lantern to illuminate the path for attainment beyond the current construct of circumstances. Self-value, the acknowledgment of one's will to choose, and empowerment to seek fulfillment for self in the world as an individual, defines an individual's perception of sovereignty.

Sovereignty is the recognition that one is an individual, separate from other individuals in the world and the narrative of experiences that perpetuate in a life. Sovereignty is the compliment to collective unity in the dualistic design of current consciousness. Polarization is a natural occurrence to grasp understandings of the working parts within the design of duality. Yet, balance and dynamic flow in the relationship of the duality perceived, consistently reveal themselves as the most successful approach to harnessing both polarities. Therefore, sovereignty and collective unity are essential to fulfillment and the evolution of consciousness within self. Acknowledging the will and worthiness to stand in sovereignty and to work with co-creating in collective unity supports the evolution of consciousness for self, others, and the world. The constellation effect harnesses and reveals the balance or imbalance for how an individual is aligned in the dance of self-value, acknowledgment of will, and empowerment to seek fulfillment. The concept of constellation is how an individual orients beliefs, thoughts, emotions, and acts in their own personal narrative as well as the interpersonal relationships with other individuals, endeavors, or inanimate aspects of experience.

As polarization occurs within oneself, relationships with others, or to the world, the degree of polarity greatly affects the whole of global consciousness. Perceptions of entitlement, selfishness, victimization, and acquiescence, conformity, or denial are just some of the concepts and feelings that arise to be faced, clarified, and responded to, in order to work out the experience of sovereignty and collective unity, self-value and collective value, worthiness and feelings of defeat. Moving through the smoke and mirrors effect of individual and collective projection is imperative to harmonizing the constructs of everyone's future. Finding clarity and heart wise solutions for the path forward requires stepping out of the milieu of internal and external fears, judgments, and reactionary behaviors. Centering in the core of one's deepest values for self, others, and the world, as having meaning and purpose to understand, is an act of honoring the authentic self. Honoring the authentic self does not require input from others or the narratives of the world. Listening to the profound wisdom of the authentic self creates sacred relationship based in the strength of self-love and self-worth. This perpetuates the empowerment of one's gift of life and creativity.

Here in the forge of that sacred self, an individual may nourish, purify, regenerate, and redesign the constructs of their personal narrative and work to manifest the balance of perceptions within self, interpersonal relationships, or projections from collective consciousness. The authentic self accepts its own worthiness and the worthiness of others. The balanced truth of self-value, value of others, and the value of the world is applied through acts of witnessing, compassion, and empowering efforts to attain harmony and fulfillment for the sovereign self and the collective. Understanding and harnessing the polarities of the mind is extracurricular and simultaneously informative to the alignment of an individual's acknowledgment for their own self-value, will in choice, and empowerment to seek fulfillment. Regardless of the outcomes, environmental factors, and beliefs of others in an individual's personal narrative, the power of worthiness is the light of vitality crystallized within, by the acknowledgment and acceptance of oneself.

~Listen deep to the fire in the forge of your heart. Attend to the essence of self-love and purpose. Mend the mind to reveal the magic of will and embrace sacred relationship with the authentic self. ~

XXVI

✤

Lightheartedness in Times of Hardship

"*Ser Feliz Es Una Decision*" is the graffiti tag on a concrete wall in a lower socioeconomic neighborhood in Cancun, Mexico. "*To be happy is a decision.*" This phrase ripples with deep wisdom in times of hardship. It intersects with Buddhist philosophies about "*Life as all forms of suffering.*" and Vedic Scriptures that say, "*The pain is inevitable the suffering is optional.*" Statements like these may seem empty and myopic to an individual overwhelmed with emotional, mental, and/ or physical hardship, but are they really naïve philosophies? Is all of life suffering when laughter, excitement, creativity, and success are existing possibilities? Is pain truly inevitable or is it one's perception of pain that is inevitable? The choice to be happy in the face of loss, failure, and decisive conflict throughout life requires the will to differentiate circumstances from a personal and impersonal view-point. This helps one gain perspective from emotional subjectivity and mental objectivity in order to strategize the steps for resolve, healing, and success. To move beyond the turmoil of hardships, the practice of acknowledgment and gratitude for the teachings of change and co-creativity must be balanced with the experience of oppression and demotivation. Herein, exists a doorway to uplift the heart and mind, to release the energy of consumption, and direct one's attitude and intention for creative solutions that are founded in worthiness and appreciation.

Lightheartedness is an invocable experience of feeling and thought. The science of meditation and attention to positive moments, affirmations, and actions such as smiling and laughing, even when the day or life feels heavy, activates brain chemicals that augment emotional states. How does it feel when you are lost in thought, walking down the street, and look up to smile at someone passing by who returns this smile of acknowledgment? How does it feel to push laughter out of your body when you are alone? Does it feel silly or empowering? If it feels silly you are still experiencing a lighter state of witnessing self than being caught up in the weight of cycling thoughts and emotions. It is important to engage that silly inner child during hardship. The inner child is where the vitality and passion we seek is found, in order to break past demotivating and judgmental blocks that come with processing life conflicts. This wholesome connection supports a way back into a flexible mindset. Being flexible is how one bends with the winds of fate or the consequences accepted by choices made of an individual's own free will. This opens the perceptive possibilities for creative solutions that expand one's vision for direction, to move beyond a predicament and enable graceful acceptance for the trade-offs that come in every choice one makes, as they navigate their own personal narrative.

Other considerations to shift mood include cathartic music in alignment with emotions for honor and release followed by reflective or uplifting music that inspires positive emotional states. Spending time with people, animals, or in nature that create opportunities to share the comfort of stillness or to feel loved and appreciated, can help redirect entrenched judgments about one's experience. Offering oneself these opportunities may benefit a sense of reprieve that brings objectivity. Reading or watching comedy can also be very soothing to a depressed and depleted individual if they are still above the threshold of apathy. When an individual is navigating their personal narrative with apathy the opportunity to move through life with curiosity, gratitude, and an openhearted mind are deferred. Apathy is the antithesis to passion and receptivity when an individual is depleted to the point of uncaring or choosing apathy to resist affectation. The point is not distraction. It is about intentional receptivity to the many shades of life and welcoming in the differentiation of an individual's personal and impersonal perceptions that can be cultivated as a reflex in the practice of uplifting.

Life is a practice. All the way through we meet challenges again and again that can frame behaviors detrimental to clarity, balance, lightheartedness, and successful creativity for self-fulfillment. Acknowledging it's a practice gives an individual the opportunity to choose what the goal of the practice is and how to live by this. Do you prefer to live in the practice of fatalism and victimhood and the practice of enduring suffering no matter the depletion of your sense of self? Or do you prefer to live in the practice of free will and discernment, and the practice of transmutation for gratitude and empowerment? The choice is up to you. Practicing lightheartedness in times of hardship may feel daunting or irresponsible to some. The lens of subjectivity, taking all of life personally and the lens of objectivity, removing self from any experience of affectation, are the extremes to subdue. Life is not personal or impersonal, alone. One's experience of circumstances will always present both personal and impersonal influences for perception.

How an individual is aligned, inherently and philosophically, on this spectrum dictates the perceptions brought into emotional and reflective awareness. Impersonal factors are discerned by understanding intentionality or un-intentionality from external factors or persons beyond an individual's control. It is key to understand what thoughts or emotions are superimposed but not originating from self and the framework of circumstances causing compensatory conflict for anyone subject to those circumstances. By witnessing one's orientation, historically and in the current context of experience, an individual may consider the practice of weighing personal and impersonal perceptions, in order to balance the act of honoring evoked emotions while transmuting impersonal factors that block the path to fulfillment and resolve.

In any given circumstance when conflict arises, there are wants and there are needs. The array of misperceptions, projections, assumptions, and ideals are there to be reckoned with. All of these components must be processed and sorted to evaluate factual evidence and differentiate philosophical truths. Depending on an individual's alignment, the pain and suffering felt from a lack of fulfilled needs and wants will perpetuate if clarity is mired by misperceptions that are caused by unacknowledged blocks and clinging to what is unfulfilled. Working with absolute needs is essential to defining the boundaries of the conflict and how to proceed with creative solutions in order to seek the achievement of those needs. Defining wants feels more negotiable to a circumstance than essential needs. Every individual must assess with willful honesty in self what defines a true need versus a want.

Whether an individual is aligned to the philosophy of resistance and loss or the philosophy of learning receptivity and gains, will determine the default mindset and behaviors they engage an experience from. Fairness is a philosophical ideal in human conceptualization that reaches for balance, but balance is a dance of trade-offs in the navigation of one's personal narrative. Fairness is dependent on shared perceptions of balance and the defined rules of engagement in society or in every relationship that is agreed upon. Without agreements for definition on equalization or mutuality, fairness cannot be met. This leaves the dance of trade-offs and the acts of free will as the primary framework for finding lightheartedness in times of hardship. Resilience is marked by healthy passion and will power that require a flexible mindset for adaptation in factors beyond one's control. It requires receptivity to creative solutions, perceptible in the field of knowing, that empower acts of transmutation and self-fulfillment. When given attention, the authentic self will radiate light and clarity to disperse the storms of confusion, resistance, and despair. The practice of life is what forms the foundation and constitution of the self, again and again. Rebirthing one's constitution beyond foundational childhood influences and experiential outcomes from any phase of living is made possible for every being that acknowledges a choice in how they perceive, manage, and accept the trade-offs in times of hardship.

How do you want to live life? How do you want to perceive yourself when you reflect on your choices in life and the foundation of that constitution that defines you in the world? The origin of this truth comes from within. It is nestled in the softness of the childlike heart, enveloped by the weathered hands of a wise elder. The inner spark of creativity in every individual is the same. How it is nourished, formed, illuminated, and radiated is up to you.

~Choose laughter with tears of appreciation, smile upon your own self worth, and claim your story with curious reflection. Embrace graceful knowing that you define the most essential trade-offs of your own heart and soul.~

Meditations for Personal Healing & Empowerment

Meditations for Personal Healing & Empowerment

It is recommended that you consider recording meditation transcripts in a Voice Memo App and listen to them in order to achieve an empowering self-guided visualization.

Stay tuned for downloadable audio meditations by the author at www.faizhealing.net/reflectionsblog

XXVII

⚬⚬⚬

Lotus Blessings
Empowerment Meditation

Standing with feet shoulder width apart, close your eyes and take a moment to notice your breath. Feel your feet magnetized to the earth with a lightness in gravity. Deepen your next inhale for 5 counts through the nose, exhaling for 7 counts out of the nose.

Continue to breathe this way as you release any attachment to thoughts or feelings cycling within. See your vessel illuminated in a nature sanctuary of your choosing. Notice the feel of the ground, the climate, any sounds, or other elements in your surroundings.

Begin to notice the warmth and tingling in the soles of your feet. Violet orbs begin to grow and expand on the top of your feet as the white roots of light extend deep into the earth, calling in the essence of Source for new life and strength to grow.

The petals of lotus begin to unfold on the surface of your

feet-- with a bright white and golden center, defining the grace and confidence in each step forward beyond this moment.

Inhale the light up from your toes, through your legs, and into your pelvic bowl.

Continue raising that light up into your heart where it branches into your neck and head- and across the shoulders, down the arms, to the palms of your hands- reaching each fingertip.

Exhale, feeling the orbs of light birthing from your palms and unfurling into yellow and white tipped lotus flowers with a center of violet and pink. Holding the light of love and gratitude, breathe into the sensations vibrating your heart and mind.

Acknowledge the gifts you carry to offer the world, the one's you care for, and to yourself.

Create the sound "ssssshhhhh"??? for approximately 9 counts.

Call up the laughter in your deepest well of beingness and let it magnify this moment of being in body, in witness to self, with compassion for the path ahead- as it is revealed to you.

Deep breath in- Exhale into the environment around you, radiating that light to all those that you love and that love you.

Deep breath- Exhale back into the core of your being, slowly opening your eyes.

Awaken, into this time and space.

XXVIII

❧

Meditation for Aligning with Gratitude for your Earthen Body

For the following meditation find a comfortable position and settle in with 5 deep breaths, inhaling and exhaling, each to a count of 5 in duration.

Turn your focus inward to the center of you body, the core of your essence where all the sacred organs are contained and protected. Take a moment to feel the warm rhythms of vitality and function. Inspiring-Digesting-Absorbing-Assimilating-Directing-Cleansing-and Eliminating. Sorting all that does and does not serve you. Consider the wonder for all these working systems communicating together to fortify your liveliness and embodiment.

-------Thank your organs for taking care of this body and

sustaining your capacity to experience the world around you.--------

Let your attention drift to your limbs, feeling the tone of your muscles and joints bestowing mobility and the opportunity to move in and out of experiences- to give and to receive- to touch, grasp, and stabilize when you feel unsteady. See the energetic awareness of your limbs in tune with the extensions of your mind, seeking to embrace and attain. Consider all they have helped you to accomplish in your life.

------Thank your limbs for all the work they do and for all that you give and receive with them. -------

See the flow of your blood, lymph. And light moving through the vessels and tissues of your body as a whole now. Gazing as a witness on the beauty of this form and feeling- the ambience of gratitude- circulating and brightening within and around you. Follow the line of your eyebrows- nose- cheekbones- jawline- and lips--

Follow the ridge of your collarbone from shoulder to shoulder and outline the borders and boundaries of your physical form from there.

Acknowledge the sacredness of this form in all it offers you, feeling your feet stable and grounded on the earth- your heart open with love and compassion- your mind enlightened by the sun in all its vitality. Breathe in the inspiration of creation. Breathe out gratitude and acceptance.

Continue to breathe in and out for 5 full breaths. Feeling them enter through the crown of the head and move through you to the tips of your fingers and toes.

When you are ready slightly open your eyes and wiggle your fingers and toes.

Move and stretch your limbs and lightly massage your belly with sweeping clockwise motions from the right to left side of your torso. Massage your face and scalp- finishing with 3 taps lightly over the heart or sternum.

XXIX

⚜

Meditation for Building Self-Trust

Take a deep breath in and feel where it goes. Does it feel full or shallow?

-Exhale- Breathe in again- expanding and holding that breath a little more. Feel where the resistance occurs in your body. Do you feel areas opening and letting go or does it feel stuck?

-Exhale- Inhale- again and let your breath come in and out like a long easy tide coming into shore.

Each inhale should be at least 5 counts and each exhale at least 6 counts. Sit in this cycle of breathing for 13 breaths.

Then turn your focus to the central column of your body. Sense the strength of your borders and boundaries around you and the peace of being within them during this precious moment of self-tending.

See a blue light brightening in the cord of your spine from crown to root. Let it expand gradually in the center of your torso between your belly and your heart.

Let your minds eye rest in the center of this blue orb, honoring the quiet stillness of just being. As thoughts or feelings arise, let them fade back into the ocean of yourself with each exhale. Stay here as long as you feel called.

When you sense the light motivate and shift into active mind, bring your awareness back to your center just below the belly button. Acknowledge the fire- beautiful rays of red, orange, and yellow dancing up from the root of your spine.

Let yourself harness that raw energy and align it with the cooling peacefulness of that blue light- filling the rest of your limbs and body with vitality.

State out loud:
" I am the keeper of wisdom within me. I know the truth of my own heart.
I am the keeper of wisdom within me. I am open to receive the truth of my own heart.
I am open to receive the truth of my own heart."

Inhale deeply- letting these words share their power with every piece of your body, mind, and spirit.

Move through a cycle of 3 breaths, making an agreement with yourself to honor this declaration with intention and to carry this mantra with you in every moment forward.

XXX

❦

Meditation for Being One with your Authentic Self

Take a moment to feel yourself in the position you have chosen. Feel the thoughts, emotions, pleasure or discomfort, in your body.

Adjust and align yourself as needed and allow a stillness to come with quieting presence. A presence that acknowledges your heart and your mind that acknowledges the sensations of your physical body without judgment or impulse to change anything.

Inhale deeply- Exhale fully. Inhale deeply again- Exhale fully. Allow your breath to carry itself in this deeper tidal flow- in the rhythm of your own being.

Let the stillness expand within and around you, welcoming your spirit in to be seen and heard- the light and the shadows cast from your dynamic radiance, all the parts of your conscious and unconscious self, presenting in this moment of profound unity.

If judgments, observations, or emotions arise take note of them and let the light of your highest self embrace them with compassion. Let the wisdom of your shadows reveal to you the light within them, even if its only a feeling.

Listen for as long as you are called to what you need to hear about the truth of who you are. Let your highest self show you that you are love, you are worthy, and you will always be enough.

Feel the sensations of your beingness as you fully open to unite with your most authentic self in the now of your life. Joining mind, heart, and hands to magnify the continuity of your spirit in this vessel with gratitude and confidence as you journey onward in this path of incarnation.

Sense the trust in your heart and the strength in this rooted self – pulling you into alignment between earth and sky- as an integrated, consolidated, and distinguished authentic self- Clear in mind, heart, and spirit- present in this time and space.

XXXI

❦

Rainbow Light Infusion Meditation

Close your eyes or soften your gaze. Inhale, deep to the core of your spine, exhaling up through the crown of your head and down into the root of your tailbone.

Feel the expansion of the breath feeding each and every cell with vitality.

See the light in your belly, glowing creamy orange, red, and yellow-ascending up into your heart to meet the radiant greens, deep blues, and violets.

Continue inhaling and exhaling to the count of 7, exploring the dance of colors.

Let these rays of light fuse and radiate outward from the center of your heart and belly in a burst of rays embracing your vessel-protecting, attuning, and aligning the web of your heart and mind in body.

Take a moment to witness the sensations as you bask in this light bath that is you.

Feeling centered in the pillar of your spine, Resound the tone of "Ohm".

The tone of Ohm is a low guttural note achieved through calling up sound from your lower belly to the back of your throat.

Feel free to tone the sound of "Ohm" 3-5 times or as long as you feel called.

When you are ready, take a soothing inhale through the nose and exhale out the mouth. Let your gaze remain soft as you sense your feet firmly on the earth- stable and supported in the path forward.

Acknowledge your heart and mind- clear and present- in this time and space.

XXXII

〰️

Meditation for Graceful Acceptance

Centering your awareness behind your eyes. Feel the warmth of blood flowing through your skin, through your mind, and through your limbs. Letting the tide of your breath be even, slow, and deep.

Take a deep breath in-
Imagine your body surrounded by a soft white light- reflecting in the pores of your flesh like crystals shimmering in the light of the sun. Feel the sanctuary in this moment to look inward and be one with all the parts of self.

Let stillness fill you- releasing any thoughts or judgments that burden the mind and heart.

Take a deep breath in and exhale fully- pushing the breath until your belly slightly contracts and inhale again
Filling your belly to a point of comfort. Sense the weightlessness

of your physical vessel hovering just above the earth as you sit or lay in this sanctuary of self-

Exhaling any resistance, fears, confusion, grief, or dissonance--- and inhaling the sweetness of vitality and nourishment your spirit requires in this moment.

Repeat the affirmation three times:

"I release that which no longer serves me. I honor the wisdom of this experience with graceful acceptance. I open my heart to listen to my authentic self. Beyond judgment, fear, and resistance I move forward on the path of passionate existence."

Inhale deeply—and exhale fully—for 5 breaths

Let the image of your elder self come into view. See the quiet smile and radiant warmth in your face and posture. Your elder self has a message for you. Listen without expectation to the message that will support you most during this time.

Take a deep breath and slowly open your eyes to a soft gaze. Know that you can carry this message with you and return to this space when called.

As you get up from this meditation, lightly shake your limbs- bending your knees, rotating your wrists, ankles, and neck from side to side. Deepening your awareness into the earth beneath your feet and grounding in with the hands as well before moving forward on your path in this time and space.

About the Author: Then to Now

Julie Hightman began her journey as a Holistic Healthcare Professional in 2004. Her focus on volunteering and treating addiction, abused women, veterans returning from war, and hospice have brought her many stories and experiences as a witness and facilitator of healing. Her offerings as a writer and an artist are another essential outlet for the passion and creativity she seeks to share with the world.

Author of the Poetry Collection "Seasons of Witnessing" and the Memoir "Why Birds Sing at Dawn: Embracing Death and Change as Transformation," Julie's message to the world is always one of curiosity, cathartic surrender, self-refinement, and the practice of savoring gratitude.

If you want to know more about her offerings or stay connected to new reflections and empowering practices, stay tuned via
www.FaizHealing.net
www.FaizHealing.com